THE LAWS

OF

WAR ON LAND

(WRITTEN AND UNWRITTEN)

BY

THOMAS ERSKINE HOLLAND, K.C.

OF LINCOLN'S INN
CHICHELE PROFESSOR OF INTERNATIONAL LAW AND DIPLOMACY
D.C.L., AND FELLOW OF ALL SOULS COLLEGE, OXFORD
HON. LL.D., F.B.A.
MEMBRE DE L'INSTITUT DE DROIT INTERNATIONAL

THE LAWBOOK EXCHANGE, LTD.
Clark, New Jersey

ISBN 978-1-58477-659-8

Lawbook Exchange edition 2009, 2019

The quality of this reprint is equivalent to the quality of the original work.

THE LAWBOOK EXCHANGE, LTD.
33 Terminal Avenue
Clark, New Jersey 07066-1321

Please see our website for a selection of our other publications and fine facsimile reprints of classic works of legal history:
www.lawbookexchange.com

Library of Congress Cataloging-in-Publication Data

Holland, Thomas Erskine, Sir, 1835-1926.
The laws of war on land (written and unwritten) / by Thomas Erskine Holland.
p. cm.
Originally published : Oxford : Clarendon Press ; New York : H. Frowde, 1908.
Includes bibliographical references and index.
ISBN-13: 978-1-58477-659-8 (cloth : alk. paper)
ISBN-10: 1-58477-659-5 (cloth : alk. paper)
1. War (International law) I. Title.
KZ6385.H65 2009
341.6'3--dc22

2008052813

Printed in the United States of America on acid-free paper

THE LAWS

OF

WAR ON LAND

(WRITTEN AND UNWRITTEN)

BY

THOMAS ERSKINE HOLLAND, K.C.

OF LINCOLN'S INN
CHICHELE PROFESSOR OF INTERNATIONAL LAW AND DIPLOMACY
D.C.L., AND FELLOW OF ALL SOULS COLLEGE, OXFORD
HON. LL.D., F.B.A.
MEMBRE DE L'INSTITUT DE DROIT INTERNATIONAL

Oxford
AT THE CLARENDON PRESS
LONDON AND NEW YORK: HENRY FROWDE
ALSO SOLD BY
STEVENS & SONS, LIMITED, 119 & 120 CHANCERY LANE, LONDON

1908

HENRY FROWDE, M.A.
PUBLISHER TO THE UNIVERSITY OF OXFORD
LONDON, EDINBURGH
NEW YORK AND TORONTO

PREFACE

The evolution of customary rules, designed to lessen the sufferings resulting from warfare, was the earliest achievement of the nascent science of International Law.

It is, therefore, not surprising that, when, in quite recent times, efforts began to be made to formulate in writing the precepts of that science, by the quasi-legislative action of the civilized Powers of the world in Conference assembled, the first topic so to be dealt with should be the conduct of war.

The Conventions by which this process of international legislation has been effected, so far as it relates to hostilities taking place on land, are textually set out, with all needful explanatory matter, in the body of this work. I have suggested, for reasons explained in an Introductory Chapter, that they might be collectively described as the "Hague Code of Land Warfare".

The Code is, however, as yet, far from dealing with all the points upon which guidance is provided by International Law, and its method is, as might, indeed, be expected from the piecemeal manner of its composition, by no means all that could be wished.

While, therefore, making use of the provisions of the Conventional Acts, as far as they go, I have incorporated them in a Code of my own, designed to exhibit, in a series of continuous articles, all the well-established rules of International Law with reference to War on Land, whether supported only by the tacit consent of Nations, or expressly sanctioned by treaties of general obligation.

I venture to think that the book, which has involved far more labour than might be supposed without close examination of its contents, may be found useful to the military profession, as well as to others who have occasion to study the branch of International Law of which it treats. I may even hope that, when, six or seven years hence, a third Peace Conference may take in hand the revision of portions of the work of its predecessors, some of the observations made in the following pages upon the system and language of the Conventions, as they stand, may be thought not altogether unworthy of attention.

It must be borne in mind that no final statement is as yet possible of the extent to which the newer Acts may ultimately become, by ratification or accession, of general obligation (see Appendix No. IV, and especially the note on p. 138). In the mean time, certain articles of these Acts from which important minorities have dissented, or which appear to be otherwise unworkable, have been printed within square brackets, and are catalogued in the Index as "apocryphal".

T. E. H.

August 8, 1908.

CONTENTS

APPENDICES

Appendix III.

Appendix IV.

INTRODUCTORY CHAPTER

THE conduct of warfare is governed by certain rules, commonly spoken of as "the laws of war", which are recognized as binding by all civilized nations. The laws of war:

These rules, which derive their origin partly from sentiments of humanity, partly from the dictates of honourable feeling, and partly from considerations of general convenience, have grown up gradually, and are still in process of development. They have existed, till comparatively recent times, only as a body of custom, preserved by military tradition, and in the works of international jurists. Their authority has been derived from the unwritten consent of nations, as evidenced by their practice. un-written,

On many points, the rules of international law which relate to war on land have still to be gathered from unwritten custom and tradition; but, within the last forty years, attempts of two kinds have been made to deal with the topic in a more authoritative manner.* written.

* See the present writer's *Studies in International Law*, 1898, ch. iv, "The progress towards a written Law of War."

National manuals.

In the first place, many nations, following the example set by the United States in 1863, have issued instructions to their respective armies, in accordance with what have been supposed by the several Governments to be the rules in question. These instructions are, of course, authoritative only for the troops of the nation by which they are issued, and differ considerably one from another.*

International quasi-legislation.

But something more was long felt to be desirable. In the second place, therefore, attempts were made, with varying success, to systematize the laws of war by international discussion, and to procure the general acceptance of a uniform code of those laws by international agreement. Thus it has come to pass that the greater bulk of the rules applicable to this topic, as newly defined and amplified by conferences of delegates duly accredited by the various Powers, have now been expressed in diplomatic Acts, which have received the formal assent of so large a number of States recognized as members of the Family of Nations, as to constitute, beyond question, a body of written International Law, of general obligation, except on a few points, as against a few dissentient Powers.

This process, commencing with the Convention of Geneva, in 1864, and since intermittently continued,

* For some account of these national bodies of instructions, see *Studies, u. s.* and *infra,* Appendix I. The British Government, which had long preferred in such matters to "trust to the good sense of the British Officer", was at last induced to alter its policy, and in 1904 issued, "for the information of H.M. land forces," the "Handbook" prepared by the present writer.

has, for the present, culminated in the results achieved by the Peace Conference of 1907.

The Hague Convention No. iv.

Among the agreements thus concluded, the principal, and central, place must be assigned to the Hague Convention No. iv of 1907, "concerning the laws and customs of war on land" (a re-affirmation, with some slight improvements, of Convention No. ii of 1899). Taken together with certain other diplomatic Acts, about to be mentioned, to which it refers, or by which it is otherwise supplemented, this Convention, with its annexed *Règlement*, may fairly be regarded as an approximately complete statement of the international law of war on land. It might, perhaps, be not inappropriately described as the "Hague Code of Land Warfare".

The other diplomatic Acts, which must be read as incorporated in, or as supplementary to, the principal Convention, are the following, viz.:

The Hague Convention No. iii.

The Hague Convention No. iii of 1907, "concerning the commencement of hostilities." *

The Geneva Convention.

The Geneva Convention of 1906 (superseding that of 1864), "for the improvement of the condition of the wounded and sick in armies in the field."

The St. Petersburg Declaration.

The St. Petersburg Declaration of 1868, "concerning the prohibition of explosive bullets in time of war."

* It may be observed that the Hague Convention No. iii, the Declaration of St. Petersburg, and the three Hague Declarations apply also to war at sea; as do some of the provisions of the Hague Convention No. v, though it is professedly concerned only with war on land.

The three Hague Declarations.

The THREE HAGUE DECLARATIONS of 1899 (the first of which, having expired by the lapse of the five years for which it was originally made operative, was renewed, with some dissentient voices, in 1907, "till the termination of the third Peace Conference"). These respectively prohibit: (i) "The launching of projectiles and explosives from balloons, or by other analogous new methods"; (ii) "The employment of projectiles the sole object of which is to spread suffocating or harmful gases"; (iii) "The employment of bullets which expand or flatten easily in the human body, such as bullets with a hard casing, which does not entirely cover the core, or is pierced with incisions."

The Hague Convention No. v.

The HAGUE CONVENTION No. v of 1907, "On the rights and duties of Neutral Powers and individuals in land warfare." *

Criticisms:

Since wholesale quasi-legislation of this sort is somewhat of a novelty in the history of International Law, it may be worth while here to indicate what seem to be defects in the drafting of the Acts in question.

Diplomatic formulae should have been severed from rules of law.

(1) It is to be regretted that in only one of them, viz. in the Hague Convention No. iv, have the formulae of usual occurrence in all treaties, as to Powers represented, Plenipotentiaries, date and scope of operation, denunciation, ratification, and the like, been kept apart from provisions promulgating new rules of law.

* For some account of the historical antecedents of the abovementioned eight diplomatic Acts, see *infra*, Appendix II; for texts, Appendix III; and for lists of the Powers parties to these Acts, and to those which they supersede, Appendix IV.

It would be preferable, in every case, to insert rules of this sort, or, at any rate, those bearing directly on the conduct of warfare, in a detached *Règlement*, such as that annexed to the above-mentioned Convention, suitable for communication, disencumbered of alien matter, to troops and others, who have no concern with the mechanism of diplomacy.*

Duties of Governments and of troops should have been kept apart

(2) It is inconvenient that rules intended to serve for the guidance of armies in the field should be intermixed, as is the case in most of these Acts, with rules relating to the duties of belligerent Governments at home. As instances of this error take clause (*h*) of Art. 23 of the Hague *Règlement*, which seems to require the Signatories to legislate for the abolition of an enemy's disability to sustain a *persona standi in iudicio*. Arts. 23, 27, and 28 of the Geneva Convention create a similar duty to legislate; and many of the articles of the Hague Convention No. v deal with obligations of States, as opposed to those of individuals.

* This method was followed, both in 1899 and in 1907, in the Hague Convention "on the laws and customs of war on land"; though, apparently, by something in the nature of a happy accident; having been, it is said, suggested only by a wish to avoid giving offence to certain susceptibilities. See M. Renault in the *Actes de la Conférence*, 1899, p. 196, where he maintains that this arrangement "n'enlève rien au caractère obligatoire des règles contenues dans cette annexe". The present writer was unsuccessful in urging its adoption, on the wider grounds of logic and practical convenience, in the new Geneva Convention of 1906, as it had been in the "Projet" submitted to the Conference of that year by the British Plenipotentiaries. See the *Actes de la Conférence de Genève*, 1906, pp. 57–64, 206–208. Nor was it followed in the new Hague Conventions of 1907.

Textual issue of *Règlement* should have been required.

(3) The Powers should have undertaken to promulgate the *Règlement* textually, rather than, as is now provided, to issue instructions "in conformity" with it.*

A more logical method should have been adopted.

(4) A want of logical method is also chargeable against the Hague *Règlement* itself. E.g. in Art. 23, the clause (*f*), as to fraudulent use of flags and emblems, should have followed Art. 24, which deals with "ruses de guerre"; and clause (*h*), as to an enemy's rights of action, if admissible in any case, is wholly out of place in the article in which it occurs. Many of the rules, laid down with reference apparently only to "occupied territory", are required also under other circumstances.

Provisions as to application.

The provisions contained in these Acts, as to the extent and duration of their application, must be carefully noted.†

Duration.

They all, except the Hague Declaration No. i (the

* In the Handbook prepared by the present writer, and issued by the War Office, in 1904, to the British Army, the *Règlement* was, accordingly, set out textually, with the necessary comment. The ill effect of allowing national instructions to be merely "in conformity with" the *Règlement* may be seen in the Russian instructions of the same year, which are far from adequately representing the Hague Rules. For differing views as to the obligatory force of the text of the *Règlement*, see Renault, *u. s.*; and Herschey, on the *Russo-Japanese War*, p. 271 note, citing Holls, *Peace Conference*, p. 136, Pillet, *Lois actuelles de la Guerre*, p. 452, and the *Laws and Customs of War on Land*, of the present writer, p. 2.

† For the text of these provisions, see *infra*, Appendix III. In many of the Conventions of 1907, these provisions follow a common form.

duration of which is limited, even for the Powers which accept it, as above mentioned), are, in the first instance, of perpetual obligation upon all Powers which ratify, or accede to, them.

Denunciation.

They all, however, except the Declaration of St. Petersburg, contain a clause enabling any Power to withdraw itself from any Act to which it is a party, by sending to the proper quarter a notice of "denunciation", which will, however, not produce its effect till one year after it has been received.

Notices of ratification, accession, or denunciation must be forwarded, with reference to the Geneva Convention, to the Government of Switzerland at Berne; and with reference to the Hague Conventions and Declarations, to the Government of the Netherlands at The Hague. No place is indicated for the receipt of accessions to the Declaration of St. Petersburg.

Application restricted.

Each of the Acts contains a clause making it applicable only as between Powers which are parties to it, and only when all the belligerent Powers are parties.

When operative.

The Hague Conventions Nos. iii, iv, and v, as also the Convention of Geneva, come into force, for Powers ratifying or acceding, sixty days after the ratification or accession has been duly received. The St. Petersburg and Hague Declarations come into force immediately on receipt of ratifications or accessions.

Superseding earlier Acts.

The Hague Convention No. iv of 1907, with its annexed Regulations, and the Geneva Convention of 1906, for Powers ratifying, or acceding to them, replace respectively the Hague Convention No. ii of 1899, with its annexed Regulations, and the Geneva Convention of 1864, for Signatories of those Acts. Powers signatory of those Acts, but not of the Acts which supersede them, remain bound by the earlier Acts.

The object of this work.

The object aimed at in the present work is to set forth, in an orderly sequence, the whole of the rules of International Law, whether written or unwritten, which govern the conduct of war on land.

The Hague Code.

What we have already ventured to describe as "The Hague Code of Land Warfare" (i. e. the Convention No. iv of 1907, with its annexed Regulations, together with the supplementary Conventions and Declarations above mentioned),* comprehensive as it is, by no means covers the whole subject. On some points, custom still remains the only guide, and there will probably always continue to be a residue of questions, the answers to which will hardly admit of being stereotyped in a written document.

Unwritten rules.

In any treatise, therefore, which attempts, however concisely, to deal with the topic in its entirety, the rules which have thus far been promulgated in a written form, by international authority, will need re-inforcement by other rules which have not yet

* It must not be forgotten that, while the Parties to the Hague Convention No. iv are bound only to issue to their armed forces "instructions in conformity with" the Regulations which are annexed to it, the Parties to the other Acts here mentioned are directly bound by the whole text of those Acts.

been so expressed. The following pages will accordingly exhibit, in a series of systematically arranged, and continuously numbered articles, accompanied by so much explanatory comment as may appear to be necessary, the international law of war, unwritten as well as written.

Authorities for written law.

Articles representing the written Law of Nations are textually reproduced from the eight diplomatic Acts, the nature of which has already been explained. First in order, come the provisions of the Hague Convention No. iii, as to the commencement of hostilities; next, certain provisions of the Hague Convention No. iv, as to the application of the Regulations which are annexed to it; then the fifty-six articles of those Regulations, *seriatim*, in which, however, the Geneva Convention and the four Declarations are interpolated, in the places where they have been, as it were, incorporated by reference; and lastly come the provisions of the Hague Convention No. v, as to the relations of belligerents and neutrals.*

Apocryphal articles.

The limited obligation of certain articles, by which some of the Powers decline to be bound, is indicated by enclosing such articles in square brackets.

Authorities for unwritten law.

But, as has been already stated, the "Hague Code" does not yet cover the whole ground. Customary law must still be prayed in aid of its deficiencies, and articles purporting to express this law have, accordingly, been inserted where their presence is still required. They have been derived from the

* Articles 1–19 of this Convention were substituted in 1907 for the four concluding articles (57–60) of the *Règlement* of 1899.

most reliable sources, such as the writings of approved jurists, military and diplomatic history, and the concurrence of such national bodies of instructions as have been already mentioned.

The Hague Code in black type.

In order to enable the reader to see at a glance whether any given article belongs to the category of written, or to that of unwritten law, articles of the former kind, only, are printed in a thick black type.

Mode of citation.

Such articles are also always accompanied by a reference to the diplomatic Act in which they respectively occur. For this purpose, the several Acts are shortly cited as follows:

The Hague Convention No. iii of 1907, as (H. iii).
The Hague Convention No. iv of 1907, as (H. iv).
The Regulations thereto annexed, as . . (H. R.).
The Geneva Convention of 1906, as . . . (G.).
The St. Petersburg Declaration of 1868, as (P. D.).
The Hague Declarations of 1899, as . . (H. D.).
The Hague Convention No. v of 1907, as (H. v).

THE LAWS OF WAR ON LAND

(WRITTEN AND UNWRITTEN)

SECTION I *

GENERAL PRINCIPLES

The Object of War.

1. The object of war is to bring about the complete submission of the enemy, as speedily as may be, and with the least possible loss of life and damage to person or property. **The object of war.**

It would be generally conceded that Montesquieu was right in declaring that "nations ought in time of peace to do one another all the good they can, and in time of war as little injury as possible, without prejudice to their real interests".† Too narrow a view has, however, been taken of the object of war by those who, by way of protest against the severities countenanced by early writers,‡ would

* On the authority which can be vouched for the articles comprised in this Section, as for others, occurring in subsequent sections, which are not recorded in any general diplomatic act, see *supra* the Introduction, p. 9.

† *Esprit des Lois*, liv. i, ch. 3.

‡ As an extreme exponent of the sterner view may be taken Bynkershoek, in his *Quaestiones Iuris Publici*, lib. i, c. 1 (1727).

restrict it to a struggle between the armed forces of States. Rousseau, for instance, lays down that "war is not a relation of man to man, but of State to State, in which individuals are enemies only by accident, not even as citizens, but as soldiers".* So the Declaration of St. Petersburg, of 1868, recites "that the progress of civilization should have the effect of alleviating as much as possible the calamities of war; that the only legitimate object which States should endeavour to accomplish during war is to weaken the military forces of the enemy; that for this purpose it is sufficient to disable the greatest possible number of men".† The "Projet" submitted by Russia to the Brussels Conference of 1874, asserted that "an international war is a condition of open strife between two independent States, and between their armed and organized forces"‡; and the "Manuel", published in 1880 by the Institut de Droit International, begins with the proposition that "a state of war implies acts of violence only between the armed forces of the belligerents".§

It was in commenting upon this proposition, that von Moltke wrote to Professor Bluntschli: "The greatest kindness in war is to bring it to a speedy conclusion. It should be allowable, with that view, to employ all methods save those which are absolutely objectionable (*alle nicht geradezu verwerfliche Mittel*). I can by no means profess agreement with the Declaration of St. Petersburg, when it asserts that the weakening of the military forces of the enemy is the only lawful procedure in war. No: you must attack all the resources of the enemy's government; its finances, its railways, its stores, and even its prestige." ‖ There is much German authority to the same effect.¶

Military Necessity.

What means are justifiable.

2. Military necessity justifies a resort to all measures which are indispensable for securing this object; provided that they

* *Contrat social*, i, ch. iv.

† See *infra*, Sect. vii.

‡ See *infra*, Appendix II.

§ *Les Lois de la Guerre sur terre.* Genève, imprimerie C. Schuchardt, 1880. Translated into a great number of languages.

‖ Letter of December 11, 1880.

¶ Cf. von Clausewitz, *Vom Kriege*, 1831, c. 1; *Kriegsbrauch im Landkriege*, herausgegeben vom Grossen Generalstabe, 1902, p. 2; Lieber's *Instructions*, 1863, Arts. 15 and 30.

are not inconsistent with the modern laws and usages of warfare.

It is sufficiently obvious that the international law of war must always be the result of a compromise between what is ideally desirable and practical military requirements. So the Hague Convention No. iv is expressed to aim at diminishing the evils of war "so far as military necessities permit"; and similar provisos are of frequent occurrence in the various conventions dealing with the topic.*

A different, and much more important, function has, however, been assigned to the plea of necessity by many, and especially by German, writers. According to these authorities, the Law of War (*Kriegsrecht*) consists of two departments, one of which, the Fashion, or Custom, of War (*Kriegsmanier*, or *Kriegsgebrauch*), sets strict limits to hostile licence; while the other, the Necessity of War (*Kriegsraison, ratio belli, raison de guerre, ius necessitatis, nécessité de guerre*), recognizes exceptional cases in which those limits need not be observed, e.g., cases in which the enemy has overstepped them, or in which to observe them would endanger the army, or the object for which the war was undertaken. The distinction is an old one. See Ulr. Obrecht, *De ratione belli* (*vulgo raison de guerre*), 1697; F. W. Pestel, *De eo quod inter ius et rationem belli interest*, 1758; and the later works of Klüber, *Droit des gens*, § 243; Lueder, *Das Landkriegsrecht*, 1888, and his articles in Holzendorff's *Handbuch*, 1889, iv, §§ 65, 66; Rivier, *Droit des gens*, 1896, ii, p. 241. This view finds also clear expression in the *Kriegsbrauch im Landkriege*, of the Prussian General Staff, 1902, which, while not so cynical as von Clausewitz, speaks somewhat disparagingly of the progress of humane ideas in warfare, and, though admitting the binding force of the Geneva Convention, makes scant allusion to the Hague Regulations.

3. These laws and usages prohibit all needless cruelty, and even needless destruction of human life, or of property.

They permit, on the other hand, that an invading army may, on grounds of military necessity, devastate whole tracts of country, burning dwellings, and clearing the district of

* e. g. in the Geneva Convention, Arts. 1, 15; and in the Hague Regulations, Art. 54 (*infra* Arts. 42, 56 and 114).

supplies. In this case it is, however, the duty of the invader to make the best provision he can for the dispossessed population.

Cf. Lieber's *Instructions*, Art. 15, "Military necessity allows of all destruction of property, and obstruction of the ways and channels of traffic, travel, or communication, and of all withholding of sustenance or means of life from the enemy." Sheridan's devastation of the whole valley of Virginia was held to be justified by the surrender of General Lee, from failure of supplies. But for restrictions imposed upon the treatment of enemy property see Arts. 23 g and 47–56 of the Hague Regulations (Sections vii and ix *infra*).

Martial Law.

Martial law defined.

4. Martial law consists of such rules as are adopted, at his own discretion, by a Commander-in-Chief in the field, supplementing, or wholly or partially superseding, the laws ordinarily in force in a given district. He will, for instance, treat certain acts as offences. He will decide upon the means to be taken for ascertaining the guilt of persons charged with such acts, and the punishment to be inflicted on such persons, if found guilty. He should, so far as may be, make generally known the principles by which he intends to be guided.

"Martial law," said the Duke of Wellington in the House of Lords, "is neither more nor less than the will of the general who commands the army. In fact, martial law means no law at all. Therefore the general who declares martial law, and commands that it shall be carried into execution, is bound to lay down distinctly the rules, and regulations, and limits according to which his will is to be carried out." *Hansard*, 3rd Series, cxv. 881. "Martial law sweeps civil law by the board and takes the place of it." Speech of J. Q. Adams, Moore's *United States Arbitrations*, p. 3322.

5. "Martial law," as thus defined, must be carefully distinguished from "military law", i.e., for the British Army, that fixed body of rules, now contained in the Army Act of 1881,* as continued in force by the Army (Annual) Act, which is applicable, in peace or in war, at home or abroad, to "all persons subject to military law", and to such persons only.

Distinguished from Military law.

How limited.

6. In exercising his discretion in the administration of martial law, a commander should always be guided by the laws and customs of war, as generally accepted.

Inquiry by court.

7. Punishment under martial law should, as far as possible, be inflicted only after inquiry by a military court, convened for the purpose.

Such a court is inaccurately, though commonly, described as a "court-martial", since that term is properly applicable, in British practice, only to a court instituted under the Army Act of 1881, for dealing with offenders belonging to the British Army.

Application of martial law.

8. Martial law is most stringent where hostile armies are face to face. It may be less stringently applied in districts which are fully occupied than in those in which a renewal of hostilities may probably be expected.†

9. Martial law applies to all persons, and to all property, within the district over which it is in force, irrespectively of the nationality of such persons, except in the case of diplomatic agents accredited by neutral states to the territorial sovereign.‡

It is not usual for a British General, except in case of urgent necessity, to deal with offences by his own troops otherwise than under the Army Act.

10. In particular, a general commanding an army in the field has, during the continuance of the war, an absolute right

* 44 & 45 Vict. c. 58.

† As to "occupied territory", see *infra*, Sect. ix.

‡ As to neutral persons generally, see *infra*, Sect. xi.

Deportation. to remove from any place within the sphere of his operations all persons whose presence therein is considered by him to be dangerous or inconvenient. He may deport those persons, with as little hardship as can be avoided, to such a distance as may be necessary effectually to prevent their speedy return.

Compensation was granted, but only as a matter of grace and favour, to subjects of Neutral Powers deported by the British from South Africa during the Boer War, after careful inquiry by a commission which sat in London from May to November, 1901.

Punishment. **11.** He may take stringent measures to repress all attempts at interference with his communications, by road, railway, or telegraph, as also acts of marauding or assassination.

See, for instance, Lord Roberts's Proclamations during the Boer War. *Parliamentary Paper*, 1900 [Cd. 426].

The presence of an invader a sufficient warning. **12.** The presence of an invading Army in a district is of itself, without any special warning to the inhabitants, a sufficient proclamation that the martial law of that army is in force in that district.

When sentences under should cease to be passed. **13.** No punishment should be inflicted by martial law after the termination of hostilities, and when recourse can again be had to the ordinary Courts of Justice.

Martial Law in the Home Territory.

Recourse to martial law by the home government. **14.** In time of invasion, or in expectation thereof, exceptional powers are often assumed by the executive government of a country, acting usually through its military forces, with a view to resisting the invasion or to the maintenance of good order within its own territory. The lawfulness of the measures then taken, which are conveniently, though not necessarily, preceded by a "proclamation of martial law", or some equivalent notification, is a question not merely of international law, but also, and more especially, of the national law of the country in question.

In many foreign countries the previous proclamation of a "state of siege" gives to measures afterwards taken the legality which would otherwise be wanting to them. A similar result may follow upon a "proclamation of martial law" in such British possessions as are under the direct legislative authority of the Crown.

In the United Kingdom, however, and in most self-governing British possessions, a "proclamation of martial law" operates only by way of warning that the government is about to resort, in a given district, to such forcible measures as may be necessary to repel invasion, or suppress insurrection, as the case may be. For codes of martial law issued for Cape Colony, see Parliamentary Papers of 1902 and 1903. To obviate any question as to the conformity of the measures taken for this purpose (whether or not they have been preceded by a proclamation of martial law) to the law of the country in which they have occurred, it has been usual, within the British Empire, to pass an Imperial or local Act of Indemnity, for the protection of those engaged, so far as the steps taken by them have been reasonable in character, and adopted in good faith.*

Peaceful Inhabitants.

15. Peaceful inhabitants are to be spared in person and property during hostilities, so far as military necessity and the conduct of such inhabitants will permit.† Especial care is to be taken of women and children, the sick and the aged, and protection must be given to the diplomatic representatives and consuls of neutral Powers in belligerent territory.‡ Non-combatants.

* e. g. the Cape Colony Indemnity Acts of 1900 and 1902 and the Natal Indemnity Acts of 1900, 1901, and 1908. When the exercise of martial law has been sanctioned beforehand by statute (e. g. by 39 G. III. c. 11. 1, 43 G. III. c. 17, 3 & 4 W. IV. c. 4), a subsequent Act of Indemnity is, of course, not required.

† See *supra*, Art. 2; *infra*, Art. 76, last par., and Arts. 104–112.

‡ On the position of neutral subjects not taking part in hostilities, and the extent of their liability in person and property, if resident in enemy territory, see *supra*, Arts. 9 and 10, and *infra*, Sect. xi, Arts. 136–139.

SECTION II

The Commencement of Hostilities

Declaration of War.

Declaration of war.

16. The Contracting Powers recognize that hostilities between them ought not to commence without a warning, previously given and unequivocal, which shall take the form either of a declaration of war, accompanied by reasons, or of an ultimatum, with a conditional declaration of war. (H. iii. 1.)

This rule was adopted in 1907 with a view to obviating in the future occurrences which have given rise in the past to complaints of attacks having taken place in what seemed to be a time of peace. The value of such a rule is much lessened by the failure of all efforts to graft upon it the requirement that some fixed period of time, e.g. twenty-four hours, shall intervene between the declaration and the first hostile act.

The rule, as far as it goes, follows substantially Resolutions 1 and 2 voted at Ghent in 1906 by the Institut de Droit International; not, however, Resolution 3, to the effect that "les hostilités ne pourront commencer qu'après l'expiration d'un délai suffisant pour que la règle de l'avertissement préalable et non équivoque ne puisse être comme éludée". *Annuaire,* t. xxi, p. 292.

Notification to Neutrals.

Notification to neutrals.

17. The state of war should be notified without delay to neutral Powers, and shall not produce its effects with reference to them till they have received a notification, which may even be communicated by telegraph. Neutral Powers cannot, however, plead absence of notice, if it shall be established beyond question that in fact they were aware of the state of war. (H. iii. 2.)

The last paragraph here reminds one of the distinction long ago drawn, with reference to maritime warfare, between "diplomatic notification", "notification by notoriety", and "individual warning".

SECTION III

APPLICATION OF THE HAGUE REGULATIONS

18. The Contracting Powers will issue instructions to their armed land forces, which shall be in conformity with the Regulations respecting the Laws and Customs of War on Land annexed to the present Convention. (H. iv. 1.)

The Powers to issue instructions.

These Regulations consist of fifty-six articles, which, wherever they occur in the following pages, are distinguished by the letters H. R.

19. A belligerent Party which violates the provisions of the said Regulations shall, in proper cases, be bound to make compensation. It shall be responsible for all acts committed by persons forming part of its armed forces. (H. iv. 3.)

Responsibility of belligerent Governments.

This express admission of liability relates, it will be observed, only to violations of the body of Regulations annexed to the Hague Convention No. iv. The principle would, however, be equally applicable, one would suppose, to violations of the other Conventions and Declarations relating to land warfare.

20. Until a more complete Code of the Laws of War has been issued, the High Contracting Parties deem it expedient to declare that, in cases not included in the Regulations adopted by them, populations and belligerents remain under the protection and the government of the principles of the Law of Nations, as they result from the usages established among civilized peoples, from the laws of humanity, and the requirements of the public conscience.

Saving for unwritten Rules.

They declare that it is in this sense especially that Arts. 1 and 2* of the Regulations adopted must be understood. (H. iv. *recital.*)

* i. e. those immediately following, distinguished in the continuous numeration of this work as Arts. 21 and 22.

SECTION IV

Lawful Belligerents

Lawful belligerent forces.

21. The laws, rights, and duties of war apply not only to the army, but also to militia and to corps of volunteers, which satisfy the following requirements:—

Requirements.

1. **That of being commanded by a person responsible for his subordinates;**
2. **That of having a distinctive mark, fixed and recognizable at a distance;**
3. **That of carrying their arms openly; and**
4. **That of conducting their operations in accordance with the laws and customs of war.**

In countries where militia or corps of volunteers constitute the army, or form part of it, they are included under the denomination "army". (H. R. 1.)

The object of requirement No. 2 is to draw a distinct line between combatants and peaceful inhabitants, by insisting that the former shall wear something in the nature of a uniform, which cannot readily be put on or taken off. This requirement, under the special circumstances of the case, was not insisted on during the war in South Africa.

As to the interpretation of this, and the following article, see *supra*, Art. 20. (H. iv. *recital.*)

Relaxation in favour of *levée en masse.*

22. The population of a territory which has not been occupied who on the approach of the enemy, spontaneously take up arms to resist the invading troops, without having had time to organize themselves in accordance with Article 1 (i.e. Art. 21, *supra*), shall be regarded as belligerents, if they carry their arms openly, and if they respect the laws and customs of war. (H. R. 2.)

For what is meant by "occupied territory", see *infra*, Art. 102.

Non-combatants in armed forces.

23. The armed forces of the belligerent Parties may consist of combatants and of non-combatants. In case of

capture by the enemy, both have a right to be treated as prisoners of war. (H. R. 3.)

As to persons following an army without being directly attached to it, see *infra*, Arts. 33, 83. As to persons who are entitled to greater privileges than ordinary prisoners of war, see Arts. 47–54, 58. As to persons who cannot claim to be treated as prisoners of war, see Arts. 84–87.

SECTION V

Prisoners of War

24. Prisoners of war are in the power of the hostile Government, but not in that of the individuals or corps who captured them. Prisoners and their property.

They must be humanely treated.

All their personal belongings, except arms, horses, and military papers, remain their property. (H. R. 4.)

Prisoners may, of course, be deprived for a time of the use of their property, for sufficient reasons; and it may be a question whether large sums of money found upon prisoners, or in their baggage, are, in fact, their private property.

25. Prisoners of war may be interned in a town, fortress, camp, or any other locality, and bound not to go beyond certain fixed limits; but they can only be confined as an indispensable measure of safety, and only so long as the circumstances continue which render that measure necessary. (H. R. 5.) Internment of prisoners.

The distinction here is between restriction to a specified locality and close confinement.

26. The State may utilize the labour of prisoners of war, other than officers, according to their rank and capabilities. Such labour shall not be excessive, and shall have nothing to do with the operations of war. Their labour.

Prisoners may be authorized to work for public bodies, for private persons, or on their own account.

Work done for the State shall be paid for according to the tariffs in force for soldiers of the national army employed on similar work; or, if there be none such, according to a tariff corresponding to work carried out.

When the work is for other public bodies, or for private persons, the terms shall be settled in agreement with the military authorities.

The earnings of the prisoners shall go towards improving their position, and the balance shall be paid them at the time of their release, after deducting the cost of their maintenance. (H. R. 6.)

Work even upon fortifications, at a distance from the scene of hostilities, would not seem to be prohibited by this article.

Under "public bodies" (*administrations publiques*) would be included, e. g., municipalities, companies, &c.

It is not customary in the British Army to charge the cost of maintenance of prisoners of war against their earnings, but reciprocity of treatment is expected from the other belligerent.

Their maintenance.

27. The Government into whose hands prisoners of war have fallen is bound to maintain them.

Failing a special agreement between the belligerents, prisoners of war shall be treated as regards food, quarters and clothing, on the same footing as the troops of the Government which has captured them. (H. R. 7.)

The second paragraph here must, of course, be read subject to military necessities.

Their duties.

28. Prisoners of war shall be subject to the laws, regulations and orders in force in the army of the State into whose hands they have fallen.

Their punishment.

Any act of insubordination warrants the adoption, as regards them, of such measures of severity as may be necessary.

Escaped prisoners recaptured before they have succeeded

in rejoining their army, or before quitting the territory occupied by the army that captured them, are liable to disciplinary punishment. Their escape.

Prisoners who, after succeeding in escaping, are again taken prisoners, are not liable to any punishment for their previous flight. (H. R. 8.)

Under this article prisoners may be punishable, even by death, for conspiracy or revolt.

It is here understood, though not expressed, that all necessary steps, even such as may cause death, may be taken to prevent escape.

Disclosure of name, &c.

29. Every prisoner of war, if questioned, is bound to declare his true name and rank, and if he disregards this rule, he is liable to a curtailment of the advantages granted to prisoners of war of his class. (H. R. 9.)

Release on parole.

30. Prisoners of war may be set at liberty on parole if the laws of their country authorize it, and, in such a case, they are bound, on their personal honour, scrupulously to fulfil, both as regards their own Government and the Government by which they were made prisoners, the engagements they have contracted.

In such cases their own Government is bound neither to require of, nor to accept from, them any service incompatible with the parole given. (H. R. 10.)

In the British Army only commissioned officers are allowed to give their parole for themselves or their men. The parole must not go further than a promise not to serve during the war which at the time is in progress.

31. A prisoner of war cannot be forced to accept his liberty on parole; similarly the hostile Government is not bound to assent to the prisoner's request to be set at liberty on parole. (H. R. 11.)

Breach of parole.

32. Any prisoner of war, who is liberated on parole and recaptured bearing arms against the Government to which

he had pledged his honour, or against the allies of that Government, forfeits his right to be treated as a prisoner of war, and can be brought before the Courts. (H. R. 12.)

The Courts here mentioned are military courts, constituted under the first par. of Art. 28, *supra*. Cf. also Art. 7.

Army followers.

33. Individuals who follow an army without directly belonging to it, such as newspaper correspondents and reporters, sutlers and contractors, who fall into the power of the enemy, and whom the latter thinks fit to detain, have a right to be treated as prisoners of war, provided they can produce a certificate from the military authorities of the army they were accompanying. (H. R. 13.)

Foreign officers acting as *attachés*, or as correspondents, are bound to take no part in directing the movements of the army which they follow, and if shown to have so acted will be treated as prisoners of war. If their conduct has been in conformity with the obligations of neutrality, they may be released and afforded facilities for returning to their country, on condition that they do not, without the consent of the capturing belligerent, rejoin their posts until the conclusion of the war.

Bureaux for information.

34. A Bureau for information respecting prisoners of war is instituted, on the commencement of hostilities, in each of the belligerent States, and, if it should so happen, in the neutral countries within the territory of which belligerents have been received. The duty of this Bureau being to answer all inquiries about prisoners of war, it is furnished, by the various services concerned, with all information as to internments and changes, releases on parole, exchanges, escapes, admissions into hospital and deaths; as well as with such other information as is necessary for making, and keeping up to date, a personal entry for each prisoner of war. The Bureau must note under that entry the number, the name and christian names, the age, the residence, the rank, the corps, the

wounds, the time and place of capture, of internment, of the wounds and of the death, together with any special remarks. The personal entry shall be forwarded to the Government of the other belligerent after the conclusion of peace.

It is also the duty of the Information Bureau to collect and bring together all objects of personal use, money, letters, &c., found on the battle-fields, or left by prisoners who have been released on parole, or exchanged, or have died in hospitals and ambulances, and to forward them to those interested. (H. R. 14.)

With the second par. here, cf. Art. 45 *infra* (G. 4).

35. Such Relief Societies for prisoners of war, as are regularly constituted in accordance with the law of their country for the purpose of serving as intermediaries for charity, shall receive from the belligerents, for themselves and their duly accredited agents, every facility, within the bounds of military requirements and Administrative Regulations, for the effective accomplishment of their humane task. Delegates of these Societies may be admitted to distribute relief at places of internment, as also at the halting places of repatriated prisoners, if furnished with a personal permit by the military authorities, and on giving an engagement in writing to comply with all Regulations for order and police prescribed by such authorities. (H. R. 15.)

Prisoners' relief societies.

36. The Information Bureaux shall have the privilege of free transport. Letters, money orders, and valuables, as well as postal parcels intended for prisoners of war or despatched by them, shall be free of all postal rates, alike in countries of origin and destination, and in those passed through.

Postage.

Gifts and relief in kind for prisoners of war shall be admitted free of all duties of entry and others, as well as

Gifts.

of payments for carriage by the Government railways. (H. R. 16.)

To give full effect to this article, new postal conventions would be necessary, as also, probably, fresh legislation.

Letters written to, or received for, prisoners of war are liable to such censorship as may be ordered.

The provision in the second paragraph would apply only to articles for personal use.

Pay of officers.

37. Officers taken prisoners shall receive the pay allowed to officers of the same rank of the country whose prisoners they are, the amount to be repaid by their Government. (H. R. 17.)

Unless, of course, the liability is undertaken, in the Treaty of Peace, by the other belligerent.

Religion, worship.

38. Prisoners of war shall enjoy every facility for the exercise of their religion, including attendance at their own church services, provided only they comply with the regulations for order and police issued by the military authority. (H. R. 18.)

This article cannot, of course, be fully put into execution unless a chaplain of the prisoner's own persuasion happens to be present.

Wills.

39. The wills of prisoners of war are received or drawn up on the same conditions as for soldiers of the national army.

Certificates of death, &c.

The same rules shall be observed regarding death certificates, as well as for the burial of prisoners of war, due regard being paid to their grade and rank. (H. R. 19.)

Respect should always be shown to the enemy's dead, whether they have died on the field of battle or in captivity. Care should also be taken, before burial, to preserve their regimental number, or other evidences of identity, with a view to communicating the same to the enemy's commander, or to the Bureau mentioned in Art. 34, *supra* (H. R. 14). Cf. Art. 45, *infra* (G. 4).

40. After the conclusion of peace, the repatriation of prisoners of war shall take place as speedily as possible. (H. R. 20.) Repatriation.

Some delays must, of course, occur, on account of (1) insufficiency of transport; (2) obvious risk in at once restoring to the vanquished Power the troops of which it has been deprived; (3) some prisoners being under punishment for offences committed during their imprisonment.

SECTION VI

The Wounded and Sick

41. The duties of belligerents with regard to the wounded and sick are governed by the Geneva Convention. (H. R. 21.) The Geneva Convention.

The articles which immediately follow (42–69) represent Arts. 1–28, omitting 24, of the Geneva Convention, i.e. that which was signed on July 6, 1906, and was ratified by Great Britain on April 16, 1907; superseding, for those Powers which accept it, the earlier Convention of 1864. Signatories of the earlier Convention remain bound by it, unless, and until, they become parties to the later one. For an argument to the effect that a Power signatory of the Hague Convention of 1907, does not thereby, by virtue of its 21st article, become a party to the Convention of Geneva, see the *Manuel de la Croix-Rouge*, 1908, p. 11.

42. Soldiers, and other persons officially attached to armies, who may be wounded or sick, should be respected and taken care of by the belligerent in whose power they may be, without distinction of nationality.

Nevertheless, a belligerent who is compelled to abandon sick or wounded to the enemy shall leave with them, so far as military requirements permit, a portion of his medical personnel and material to contribute to the care of them. (G. 1.)

The restrictive clause in the second paragraph here ("so far as," &c.) should be noted. No Commander is bound to leave behind, after perhaps a succession of defeats, so much of his medical personnel and material as would interfere with due provision for the needs of his own retreating army. Similar restrictive clauses ("so far as possible," &c.) occur elsewhere in the Convention; and cf. *infra*, Art. 65 (G. 25).

43. Except as regards the treatment to be provided for them in pursuance of the preceding Article, the wounded and sick of an army who fall into the hands of the enemy are prisoners of war, and the general provisions of international law concerning prisoners are applicable to them.

Belligerents are, however, free to arrange with one another such exceptional treatment or indulgences for wounded or sick prisoners as they may think desirable; in particular they shall be at liberty to agree—

To restore to one another, after an engagement, the wounded left on the field of battle;

To send to their own country any wounded and sick whom they do not wish to retain as prisoners, after rendering them fit for removal or after recovery;

To hand over to a neutral State, with its consent, the enemy's wounded and sick, to be interned by the neutral State until the termination of hostilities. (G. 2.)

It is sufficiently obvious that Commanders are "free to agree" to the courses of action here specified, as to many other courses, quite irrespectively of any such permission as is purported to be conveyed by this article. It was, however, thought desirable to suggest to Commanders ways in which they may relax, in favour of the sick and wounded, the rigour of the rules otherwise applicable to prisoners generally. Release upon parole, it will be noticed, is not suggested.

44. After each engagement the Commander in possession of the field of battle shall take measures to search for the wounded, and to cause them, as also the dead, to be protected against pillage and ill-treatment.

He shall arrange that the burial or cremation of the dead shall be preceded by a careful examination of their bodies. (G. 3.)

The original Geneva Convention contained no such provisions with reference to the dead and their identification as are found in this and the next articles; and it has been maintained that these provisions would be more appropriately placed in some collection of rules for the conduct of hostilities, such as the Regulations annexed to the Hague Convention No. iv of 1907. Cf. *Revue de Droit International*, N. S. iv. p. 311.

45. Each belligerent shall send, as soon as possible, to the authorities of the country or army to which they belong the military identification marks or tokens found on the dead, and a nominal roll of the wounded or sick who have been collected by him.

The belligerents shall keep one another informed of any internments and changes, as well as of admissions into hospital and deaths occurring among the wounded and sick in their hands. They shall collect all the articles of personal use, money, letters, &c., which shall be found on the battle-fields, or left by the wounded or sick who have died in medical establishments or units, in order that such objects may be transmitted to the persons interested by the authorities of their own country. (G. 4.)

Cf. *supra*, Arts. 34 (H. R. 14) and 39 (H. R. 19). The duties created by this article have reference, obviously, only to the dead, wounded, and sick of the enemy. The analogous duties of a belligerent with reference to his own dead, wounded, and sick, are, of course, regulated by his own law. It was not thought desirable to make the supply to troops of marks of identity internationally obligatory, as such marks might, when found by the enemy, furnish him with valuable information as to the disposition of the hostile army.

46. The military authority may appeal to the charitable zeal of the inhabitants to collect and take care of, under his direction, the wounded or sick of armies, granting to

those who shall have responded to the appeal special protection and certain immunities. (G. 5.)

Assistance rendered by inhabitants on the field of battle must be exercised under strict supervision. Opportunity might otherwise be given for robbery and for *espionnage.*

It will be noticed that this article amounts merely to a suggestion, addressed to the discretion of Commanders. The corresponding article in the original Convention, now superseded, conferred privileges upon the inhabitants which have long been considered undesirable.

Medical Units and Establishments.

47. Mobile medical units (that is to say, those which are intended to accompany armies into the field) and the fixed establishments of the medical service shall be respected and protected by the belligerents. (G. 6.)

"Mobile medical units" must be taken here to cover all organizations which follow the troops on the field of battle (described in the British Army as "bearer companies" or "field hospitals"), while "fixed establishments", which might perhaps have been better described as "fixed units", would cover "stationary" or "general" hospitals (whether actually movable or not), placed on a line of communications, or at a base.

Units of both kinds are to be "respected", i.e. not to be fired upon; and "protected" afterwards in the discharge of their duties.

Respect and protection are due to units of both kinds, irrespectively of the actual presence in them of sick or wounded. See *infra,* Art. 50.

48. The protection to which medical units and establishments are entitled ceases if they are made use of to commit acts harmful to the enemy. (G. 7.)

49. The following facts are not considered to be of such a nature as to deprive a medical unit or establishment of the protection guaranteed by Article 6:—

1. That the personnel of the unit or of the establishment is armed, and that it makes use of its arms

for its own defence or for that of the sick and wounded under its charge.

2. That in default of armed hospital attendants the unit or establishment is guarded by a piquet or by sentinels furnished with an authority in due form.

3. That weapons and cartridges taken from the wounded and not yet handed over to the proper department are found in the unit or establishment. (G. 8.)

The piquet, or sentinels, will not be prisoners of war. See *infra*, Art. 50, and cf. Art. 58.

Personnel.

50. The personnel engaged exclusively in the collection, transport, and treatment of the wounded and the sick, or in the administration of medical units and establishments, and the Chaplains attached to armies, shall be respected and protected under all circumstances. If they fall into the hands of the enemy they shall not be treated as prisoners of war.

These provisions apply to the guard of medical units and establishments under the circumstances indicated in Article 8 (2). (G. 9.)

Cf. the comment upon Art. 47, *supra*. The persons here mentioned are bound to carefully abstain not only from acts of hostility against the enemy, but also from all acts, such as transmission of letters or messages, calculated to impede the success of his operations.

Officers and men of the Army Service Corps, attached to the Army Medical Service for the whole duration of the campaign, would be among the persons contemplated by this article.

51. The personnel of Voluntary Aid Societies, duly recognized and authorized by their Government, who may be employed in the medical units and establishments of armies, is placed on the same footing as the personnel referred to in the preceding article, provided always that the first-

mentioned personnel shall be subject to military law and regulations.

Each State should notify to the other, either in time of peace or at the commencement of or during the course of hostilities, but in every case before actually employing them, the names of the Societies which it has authorized, under its responsibility, to render assistance to the regular medical service of its armies. (G. 10.)

This article makes it quite clear that Red Cross, or Aid, Societies, unless affiliated to the regular medical organization of one or other belligerent, and subject to his military law, enjoy none of the benefits conferred by the Convention.

There is indeed no principle, even of unwritten military law, according any special rights or immunities to such societies, beyond those which may be accorded to them, as a matter of grace, in consideration of their humane efforts to alleviate suffering. It makes no difference whether or not they are recognized by the Government of the State to which they belong, as available when needed for service with its own armies.

52. A recognized Society of a neutral country cannot afford the assistance of its medical personnel and units to a belligerent without the previous consent of its own Government and the authorization of that belligerent.

A belligerent who has accepted such assistance is bound, before availing himself of it, to notify his enemy of the fact. (G. 11.)

53. The persons designated in Articles 9, 10, and 11 (i.e. Arts. 50–52, *supra*), after they have fallen into the hands of the enemy, shall continue to carry on their duties under his direction.

When their assistance is no longer indispensable, they shall be sent back to the army to which they belong, or to their country, at such time and by such route as may be compatible with military requirements.

They shall then take with them such effects, instruments, arms, and horses as are their private property. (G. 12.)

Cf. *infra*, Art. 55 (G. 14), as also the comment on Art. 24 (H. R. 4).

54. The enemy shall secure to the persons mentioned in Article 9 (i. e. Art. 50, *supra*), while in his hands, the same allowances and the same pay as are granted to the persons holding the same rank in his own army. (G. 13.)

Cf. the similar provisions as to officers prisoners, in H. R. Art. 17 (i.e. Art. 37, *supra*).

This article has no application to the *personnel* of Aid Societies which are not dealt with in Art. 50, *supra* (G. 9).

Material.

55. Mobile medical units, if they fall into the hands of the enemy, shall retain their material, including the teams, irrespectively of the means of transport and the drivers employed.

Nevertheless, the competent military authority shall have the right of using the material for the treatment of the wounded and sick. It shall be restored under the conditions laid down for the medical personnel, and, so far as possible, at the same time. (G. 14.)

For the definition of "mobile medical units", see *supra*, Art. 47 (G. 6). They are to retain their material, &c., "irrespectively of its character," i. e. although portions of it have been borrowed from military units, or obtained, by requisition, from the inhabitants of the country. On "Requisitions", see *infra*, Arts. 58, 112, 139.

This article cannot be supposed to debar the capturing Commander from using, in case of necessity, some of the material of a medical unit for the benefit of his own wounded.

56. The buildings and material of fixed establishments remain subject to the laws of war, but may not be diverted from their purpose so long as they are necessary for the wounded and the sick.

Nevertheless, the Commanders of troops in the field may dispose of them, in case of urgent military necessity, pro-

vided they make previous arrangements for the welfare of the wounded and sick who are within them. (G. 15.)

Under the "laws of war", the material becomes booty, and the buildings may be used by the enemy, subject to the reservation mentioned in this article.

The provisions of this article, it must be observed, relate only to *military* establishments and material. Civil hospitals, even when State property, would be exempt from confiscation, see *infra*, Arts. 106, 116 (H. R. 46, 56).

"Fixed establishments" may comprise, according to circumstances, not only buildings, but also assemblages of tents.

57. The material of Aid Societies which are admitted to the privileges of the Convention, under the conditions laid down therein, is considered private property, and, as such, is respected under all circumstances, saving only the right of Requisition recognized for belligerents, in accordance with the laws and customs of war. (G. 16.)

The material of Aid Societies, when employed in mobile units, would, of course, be restored in pursuance of Art. 55 (G. 14). The treatment which it should receive, when employed in fixed military establishments, is not so obvious. Should it share the fate of such establishments, under Art. 56 (G. 15)? This might be a discouragement to voluntary aid. Or should it be exempt from confiscation? The latter alternative is accepted in this article, although belligerents may thus be tempted to protect material properly belonging to their medical service, by assigning it over to Voluntary Societies. On the exemption of "private property", see *infra*, Art. 106 (H. R. 46). On the right of "Requisition", see *infra*, Art. 112 (H. R. 52).

Convoys of Evacuation.

58. Convoys of evacuation shall receive the same treatment as mobile medical units, subject to the following special provisions :—

1. A belligerent intercepting a convoy may, if this is demanded by military necessity, break it up, taking upon himself the charge of the sick and wounded who are in it.

2. In this case, the duty to send back the medical personnel imposed by Article 12 (i.e. Art. 53) shall be extended to the whole of the military personnel detailed for the transport or the protection of the convoy and furnished for this purpose with an authority in due form.

The duty to restore the medical material, provided for in Article 14 (i.e. Art. 55), shall apply to railway trains, and boats used in internal navigation, which are specially arranged for evacuations, as also to the material, belonging to the medical service, for fitting up ordinary vehicles, trains, and boats.

Military vehicles, other than those of the medical service, may be captured with their teams.

The civilian personnel and the various means of transport obtained by requisition, including railway material and boats used for convoys, shall be subject to the general rules of international law. (G. 17.)

"Convoys of Evacuation" are convoys of sick and wounded in course of conveyance. This article, although it invests such convoys with privileges similar to those enjoyed by mobile units, does not enable the Commander of a besieged place to relieve the pressure on his resources, by sending out his wounded; nor does it entitle a besieger to increase that pressure by sending a convoy of wounded into the place which he is besieging. Cf. Art. 81, *comment*.

The conveyance may take place by road, by railway, or by water; but, to enjoy the benefit of this article, must not be combined with the transport of troops, or with any other military operation.

The *personnel* of the convoy may be: (1) *Medical*, such as is mentioned in Arts. 50, 51, 52 (G. 9, 10, 11), which should be restored, in accordance with Art. 53 (G. 12); or (2) *Military*, lent for transport purposes, which should be restored under Art. 55 (G. 14); or (3) *Military guards*, to be restored under Art. 50 (G. 9); or (4) *Civil, requisitioned*, to be released, if not again requisitioned by the captor, under Art. 55 (G. 14).

The material may (1) belong to the regular medical service of the enemy, or to Aid Societies recognized by him, when it should be restored, under Art. 55 (G. 14); or (2) may consist of carriages, with their teams, borrowed from military units, which are then subject to capture; or (3) may consist of things requisitioned, e. g. carriages, boats, &c., which must be restored, in accordance with Art. 55 (G. 14).

The Distinctive Device.

59. As a compliment to Switzerland, the heraldic device of the red cross on a white ground, formed by reversing the Federal colours, is retained as the emblem and distinctive device of the medical service of armies. (G. 18.)

On the adoption of this device for voluntary Aid Societies, at the unofficial conference held at Geneva in 1863, and for medical units, &c., in time of war by the original Geneva Convention of 1864, see *infra*, Appendix II.

The phraseology of this article is intended to make it clear that the device has no religious significance, such as has been attributed to it by Mohammedan troops; so much so, that although Turkey had signed the original Convention in 1865, it was thought desirable by that Power to distinguish its own medical services, in the wars of 1876 and 1897, by a red crescent, while undertaking to continue to respect the red cross in the service of the enemy.

Turkey, the only important Power not represented at the Conference of 1906, acceded to the Geneva Convention of that year, on August 24, 1907, with, however, the reservation "that its armies will use the emblem of the Red Crescent for the protection of its ambulances"; adding: "it is nevertheless well understood that the Imperial Government will scrupulously respect the inviolability of the Red Cross flag."

60. With the permission of the competent military authority this emblem shall be shown on the flags and armlets (*brassards*), as well as on all the material belonging to the Medical Service. (G. 19.)

As to flags, see *infra*, Arts. 62–64 (G. 21–23): as to *brassards* (armlets), Arts. 61, 64 (G. 20, 23). Special dimensions are now prescribed for the crosses upon vehicles used in British field service medical units.

61. The personnel protected, in pursuance of Articles 9, 10, and 11 (i. e. Arts. 50, 51, 52), shall wear, fixed on

the left arm, an armlet (*brassard*) with a red cross on a white ground, delivered and stamped by the competent military authority, accompanied by a certificate of identity in the case of persons who are attached to the medical service of armies, but who have not a military uniform. (G. 20.)

It is desirable that armlets, with a special War Office mark, should in time of war be issued under the authority of the Principal Medical Officer, and with the official stamp of the Medical Department. A Register should be kept of the names and descriptions of the persons to whom these badges have been issued. Such persons, if not wearing a military uniform, should be furnished with an official certificate, bearing a number and a date, corresponding with entries in the Register. The framing of Regulations as to the conditions upon which armlets may be issued would be within the powers conferred upon Commanders by Art. 65 (G. 25).

62. The distinctive flag of the Convention shall only be hoisted over those medical units and establishments which are entitled to be respected under the Convention, and with the consent of the military authority. It must be accom panied by the national flag of the belligerent to whom the unit or establishment belongs.

Nevertheless, medical units which have fallen into the hands of the enemy, so long as they are in that situation, shall fly no other flag than that of the Red Cross. (G. 21.)

Under a recent Order of the British War Office, the flag is, for field hospitals, to be 9 feet square, with an 8 foot red cross, and a special pole to keep it unfurled.

A rigid metallic plate might, no doubt, be substituted for a flag of the usual materials, and a lantern, showing the red cross, may take the place of the flag by night.

The explicit statement, that by "National flag" is meant the flag of the country to which a medical unit or establishment belongs, is intended to make impossible for the future the mistake which has occasionally induced a neutral medical unit, the services of which have been accepted by a belligerent, to hoist the flag of its own neutral country. See also *infra*, Art. 63 (G. 22). Cf. *Actes de la Conférence*, pp. 214–217, 263.

No national flag, it will be observed, is to be flown by a medical unit while in captivity. It may, however, be supposed that an invader will hoist his own flag, accompanied by that of the red cross, over hospitals which he may find in the territory of which he is in occupation.

63. Medical units belonging to neutral countries which may be authorized, under the conditions laid down in Article 11 (i. e. Art. 52), **to afford their services, shall fly, along with the flag of the Convention, the national flag of the belligerent to whose army they are attached.**

The provisions of the second paragraph of the preceding article are applicable to them. (G. 22.)

The only flags which, under any circumstances, can be flown by neutral Aid Societies are, it will be observed, that of the red cross, and that of the belligerent to whose army they are attached. In captivity they can fly only the Red Cross flag.

[64. The emblem of the red cross on a white ground and the words "Red Cross" or "Geneva Cross" shall not be used, either in time of peace or in time of war, except to protect or to indicate the medical units and establishments, the personnel and the material protected by the Convention. (G. 23.)]

Great Britain has not assented to this article, which presupposes the legislation promised in Arts. 68 and 69 *infra*, to which articles she is not a party. See the comment on Arts. 68 and 69 (G. 27, 28), *infra*.

65. The Commanders-in-chief of belligerent armies shall arrange the details for carrying out the preceding articles, as well as for cases not provided for, in accordance with the instructions of their respective Governments and in conformity with the general principles of the present Convention. (G. 25.)

For these "General Principles", see *supra*, Arts. 42–63 (G. 1–22). This article, it may be remarked, leaves a useful discretion to Commanders-in-chief and Governments.

66. The Signatory Governments will take the necessary measures for instructing their troops, especially the personnel protected, in the provisions of the present Convention, and to bring them to the notice of the civil population. (G. 26.)

Punishment of Abuses and Infractions.

[**68.** The Signatory Governments, in countries the legislation of which is not at present adequate for the purpose, undertake to adopt, or to propose to their legislative bodies, such measures as may be necessary to prevent at all times the employment of the emblem or the name of "Red Cross" or "Geneva Cross" by private individuals, or by Societies other than those which are entitled to do so under the present Convention, and in particular for commercial purposes as a trade-mark or trading mark.

The prohibition of the employment of the emblem or the names in question shall come into operation from the date fixed by each legislature, and at the latest five years after the present Convention comes into force. After it comes into force, it shall no longer be lawful to adopt a trade-mark or trading mark in contravention of this prohibition. (G. 27.)]

This article has not received the assent of Great Britain. See the comment on Arts. 64, *supra*, and 69, *infra*.

[**69.** The Signatory Governments also undertake to adopt, or to propose to their legislative bodies, should their penal military law be insufficient for the purpose, the measures necessary for the repression in time of war of individual acts of pillage and maltreatment of the wounded and sick of armies, as well as for the punishment, as an unlawful employment of military insignia, of the improper use of the

Red Cross flag and armlet (*brassard*) by soldiers or private individuals not protected by the present Convention.

They shall communicate to one another, through the Swiss Federal Council, the provisions relative to these measures of repression, at the latest within five years from the ratification of the present Convention. (G. 28.)]

Arts. 68 and 69 (G. 27, 28), rendering legislation obligatory within five years, are not accepted by Great Britain, nor, therefore, is Art. 64 (G. 23), by which legislation is presupposed. All three articles are therefore here enclosed in square brackets.

The British Delegation, however, obtained the insertion in the *procès-verbal* of a statement that "The British Delegates, having been unable to agree to Arts. 23, 27, and 28 of the draft Convention, have nevertheless wished to record in the *procès-verbal* their *vœu* to the following effect: They desire that the use of the distinctive sign and name of the Red Cross should be reserved, even in time of peace, by the legislation of each country to the medical service of its armies, and of the Aid Societies which are recognized and controlled by their respective Governments".

Arts. 24, 29–33, containing only general provisions as to the application of the Geneva Convention, 1906, by the Signatory Governments, are not here set out; but see *infra*, Appendix III, pp. 116–120.

SECTION VII

The Conduct of Hostilities

The Means of Injuring the Enemy.

Restrictions on means of injuring.

70. The right of belligerents to adopt means of injuring the enemy is not unlimited. (H. R. 22.)

Cf. "On mere general principles it is lawful to destroy your enemy; and mere general principles make no great difference as to the manner by which this is to be effected; but the conventional law of mankind, which is evidenced in their practice, does make a distinction, and allows some, and prohibits other, modes of destruction". Sir W. Scott, in the *Flad Oyen*, 1 Rob. 134.

Prohibited Weapons.

71. Considering that the progress of civilization should have the effect of alleviating as much as possible the calamities of war; **Arms causing needless suffering or inevitable death, not to be employed.**

That the only legitimate object which States should set before themselves during war is to weaken the military forces of the enemy;

That for this purpose it is sufficient to disable the greatest possible number of men;

That this object would be exceeded by the employment of arms which would uselessly aggravate the sufferings of disabled men, or render their death inevitable;

That the employment of such arms would, therefore, be contrary to the laws of humanity; (P. D. *recitals*.)

It is now very generally thought that clauses 2 and 3 of these Recitals are capable of being so read as to limit too narrowly the legitimate methods of making war. See *supra*, the comments upon Arts. 1 and 2; and *infra*, the Recitals of the Hague Conventions of 1907, in Appendix III.

72. The Contracting Parties engage mutually to renounce, in case of war among themselves, the employment by their military or naval forces of any projectile of a weight below 400 grammes,* which is either explosive or charged with fulminating or inflammable substances. (P. D.) † **Explosive bullets.**

[73. The Contracting Powers agree to prohibit, for a period extending to the termination of the third Peace Conference, the discharge of projectiles and explosives from balloons, or by other new methods of a similar nature. (H. D. 1, 1907.)]

This Declaration, having been originally drafted in 1899, by the first Peace Conference, to operate for five years only, expired by efflux of time. (Cf. *supra*, p. 4.) It had been ratified by almost

* i.e., approximately, 14 oz.

† For a list of the Powers, including Great Britain, parties to this Declaration, see *infra*, Appendix IV; and for its diplomatic clauses, Appendix III.

all the Powers represented, except Great Britain. As redrafted in 1907 by the second, it is to remain in force to the end of the third, Peace Conference. So many first-class Powers are, however, now opposed to its adoption, that although ratified by the United States on March 10, and signed by Great Britain on June 29, 1908, it is here enclosed in square brackets, as an indication of defective authority.* It was generally conceded at the Conference that balloons must not be allowed to attack undefended places; but it was thought that this was sufficiently provided for by the words "by any means whatever", now inserted in Art. 25 of the Hague Regulations (*infra*, Art. 80).

74. The Contracting Powers renounce the use of projectiles the sole object of which is the diffusion of asphyxiating or harmful gases. (H. D. 2, 1899.)

This, and the following, Declaration are, unless denounced, of perpetual obligation. They were ratified or acceded to by almost all the Powers represented at the Conference of 1899, except Great Britain, the United States, and Portugal, which, however, in the course of the proceedings of the Conference of 1907, signified their adhesion to both Declarations. Great Britain formally acceded to both on August 30, 1907.

75. The Contracting Powers renounce the use of bullets which expand or flatten easily in the human body, such as bullets with a hard casing which does not entirely cover the core, or is pierced with incisions. (H. D. 3, 1899.)

As to the parties to this Declaration, see comment on the preceding article; and cf. *infra*, Art. 76 (*e*) (H. R. 23 (*e*)). The United States, both in 1899 and in 1907, urged the adoption of a more comprehensive Declaration, prohibiting the employment of "balls which inflict wounds needlessly cruel, such as explosive balls, and, in general, every species of ball which exceeds the limit necessary to place a man immediately *hors de combat*".

* For a list of Powers accepting this Declaration, of which Great Britain is one of the signatories, see *infra*, Appendix IV. For the adverse attitude of Germany, &c., see the *Weissbuch*, presented to the Reichstag in December, 1907, p. 7, which states that "Germany had acceded to the agreement at the Conference, conditionally on all the great military Powers accepting the same standpoint. Since several of these Powers have objected to the renewal, Germany also will be unable to sanction it".

Certain further Prohibitions.

76. Besides the prohibitions provided by special conventions,* it is especially prohibited:— Prohibition of

(*a*) **To employ poison or poisoned arms;** Poison,

And, on analogy, it has been suggested, to spread contagious diseases.

(*b*) **To kill or wound treacherously individuals belonging to the hostile nation or army.** Assassination.

This includes not only assassination of individuals, but also, by implication, any offer for an individual "dead or alive".

(*c*) **To wound or kill an enemy who, having laid down his arms, or having no longer means of defence, has surrendered at discretion.** Refusal of quarter,

It may be a question up to what moment acts of violence may be continued without disentitling the doer to be ultimately admitted to the benefit of quarter under this clause.

An offer to surrender is frequently communicated by the hoisting of a white flag, which, however, can protect only the force by which it is hoisted.

(*d*) **To declare that no quarter will be given.** Declaration of no quarter,

(*e*) **To employ arms, projectiles, or material, of a nature to cause superfluous injury.** Superfluous injury,

Cf. Arts. 71, 75, *supra*.

(*f*)†

(*g*) **To destroy or seize the enemy's property, unless its destruction or seizure be imperatively demanded by the necessities of war.** Needless destruction of property.

The "necessities of war" may obviously justify not only the

* i. e. up to the present time, by the four immediately preceding Declarations (P. D., and H. D. 1, 2, 3).

† H. R. 23 (*f*) has been transferred to the topic of *Stratagems* (Arts. 78 and 79), to which it properly belongs.

seizure of private property, but even the destruction of such property, and the devastation of whole districts. See *supra*, Art. 3.

[(*h*) To declare extinguished, suspended, or unenforceable the rights and rights of action of the subjects adverse party. (H. R. 23.)]

This clause, suggested by Germany, if intended only for the guidance of an invading Commander, needs careful re-drafting; if, as would rather appear, it is of general application, besides being quite out of place where it stands, it is so revolutionary of the doctrine which denies to an enemy any *persona standi in iudicio*, that although it is included in the ratification of the Convention by the United States on March 10, and the signature of the same, on June 29, 1908, by Great Britain, it can hardly, till its policy has been seriously discussed, be treated as a rule of International Law. It is here, accordingly, included in square brackets.

77. It is also prohibited to a belligerent to compel the subjects of the adverse party to take part in operations of war directed against their own country, even when they have been in his service before the commencement of the war. (H. R. 23, *last par.*)

This article, drafted by Germany, was in 1907 rather awkwardly annexed to H. R. 23 (Art. 76, *supra*), in substitution for Art. 44 of H. R. of 1899, which ran as follows: "any compulsion on the population of occupied territory to take part in *military operations* against its own country is prohibited." The immunity now accorded to subjects of the invaded State is considerably greater than that guaranteed to them by the old articles. In the first place, it relates to taking part in any *operations of war*, a term supposed to cover many acts not amounting to what would be described as *military operations*. An Austrian amendment, which would have limited the exemption to taking part "as combatants", was accordingly rejected. In the second place, the subjects of that State are protected against compulsion to take part against their own country, even if they have previously been enrolled in the service of the invader.

The terminology employed is, however, still ambiguous. Would this article render unlawful any compulsion on inhabitants of occupied territory to execute urgently required works, such as,

e. g., repairs to roads or bridges, although of ultimate military utility? A still more delicate question is whether it would protect the inhabitants from being compelled to act as guides to the enemy. The practice of exacting services of this kind was reprobated by many Powers at the Conference, but is still treated as admissible in 1902, by the *Kriegsbrauch* of the Prussian General Staff, p. 48. Cf. *Weissbuch*, p. 7. It must be noted that Germany, with several other first-class Powers, declines to accept Art. 104 (H. R. 44), *infra*.

Stratagems.

78. Stratagems and the employment of methods necessary to obtain information about the enemy and the country are considered lawful. (H. R. 24.) Stratagems allowed.

Good faith must, however, always be observed with the enemy, and this article must not be taken to authorize any such acts of treachery as are expressly forbidden in Art. 76 (*b*), and in Art. 79 (H. R. 23 (*b*) and (*f*)).

79. It is, however, forbidden **to make improper use of a flag of truce, of the national flag, or the military distinguishing marks and the uniform of the enemy, as well as of the distinctive signs of the Geneva Convention. (H. R. 23 (*f*).)** Fraud forbidden.

Frederick the Great, in the 13th article of his *Principes généraux de la guerre*, enlarges on the utility of "ruses de guerre": "On prend alternativement, à la guerre, la peau de lion et la peau de renard; la ruse réussit où la force échouerait."

On flags of truce, see Arts. 88–91, *infra*. The treacherous use of a white flag as indicating a readiness to surrender is, of course, within this prohibition.

By "national flag" is, of course, meant the flag of the enemy. Cf. Art. 62, *supra* (i. e. G. 21).

Troops may sometimes be obliged by lack of clothing, and with no fraudulent intent, to make use of uniforms belonging to the enemy. Care must be taken in such cases to make alterations in the uniform which will clearly indicate the side to which those who wear it belong.

Sieges and Bombardments.

Sieges and bombardments.

80. The attack or bombardment, by whatsoever means, of towns, villages, habitations, or buildings, which are not defended, is prohibited. (H. R. 25.)

The words "by whatsoever means" were held at the Conference of 1907 to include attack from balloons. Cf. *supra*, Art. 73 (H. D. 1).

A place, although not fortified, may be bombarded if it is defended. This article is not to be taken to prohibit the use of any means for the destruction of buildings for military reasons.

A place must not be bombarded with a view merely to the exaction from it of ransom. Cf. the Hague Convention of 1907, No. ix, on bombardments by naval forces in time of war.

Warning.

81. The Commander of an attacking force, before commencing a bombardment, except in the case of an assault, should do all he can to warn the authorities of what is about to happen. (H. R. 26.)

By "assault" a surprise attack is here intended. The besieger is under no absolute obligation to allow any portion of the population of a place to leave it, even when a bombardment is about to commence.

Objects to be spared.

82. In sieges and bombardments all necessary steps should be taken to spare, as far as possible, edifices devoted to religion, art, science, and charity, historical monuments, hospitals, and places where the sick and wounded are collected, provided they are not used at the same time for military purposes.

The besieged should indicate these buildings or places by some special visible signs, which should previously be notified to the assailants. (H. R. 27.)

Pillage.

83. The giving up to pillage of a town or place, even when taken by assault, is prohibited. (H. R. 28.)

Much less may a garrison, as was at one time practised, be put to the sword for an over-obstinate defence. As to pillage, cf. Art. 107 (H. R. 47), *infra*.

Spies.

84. An individual can only be considered a spy if, acting clandestinely, or on false pretences, he obtains, or seeks to obtain, information in the zone of operations of a belligerent, with the intention of communicating it to the hostile party. Spies, who are,

Thus, soldiers not in disguise who have penetrated into the zone of operations of a hostile army to obtain information are not considered spies. Similarly, the following are not considered spies: soldiers or civilians, carrying out their mission openly, charged with the delivery of dispatches intended either for their own army or for that of the enemy. To this class belong likewise individuals sent in balloons to deliver dispatches, and generally to maintain communications between the various parts of an army or a territory. (H. R. 29.) who are not.

To claim the benefit of the second clause of this article soldiers must be in uniform.

Persons in balloons are not spies, even if engaged in observing the movements of the enemy.

The examples given in this article are not intended to be exhaustive.

85. A spy cannot claim to be treated as a prisoner of war.

Nor, according to the Prussian General Staff, *Kriegsbrauch*, p. 31, can persons assisting, or concealing, spies claim to be so treated. Frederick the Great, u. s. 14, mentions, besides ordinary spies, "doubles espions," i.e. persons employed to convey false information to the enemy, sometimes pretending to be deserters ("mentiti transfugae" in the older writers); and he confesses to having descended to forcing some respectable "bourgeois" to enter the camp of the army of his own country, under the surveillance of an enemy soldier disguised as his servant, with whom he is to return to his homestead with the required information, on pain of finding his wife and children murdered and all his belongings burnt.

Trial of spies.

86. A spy taken in the act cannot be punished without previous trial. (H. R. 30.)

The severity with which spies are treated is exercised merely to prevent their employment. The motives with which a spy has acted have therefore no bearing either way upon his treatment.

When their liability ceases.

87. A spy who, after rejoining the army to which he belongs, is subsequently captured by the enemy, is treated as a prisoner of war, and incurs no responsibility for his previous acts of espionnage. (H. R. 31.)

He may, of course, have incurred responsibility for acts of a different kind.

SECTION VIII

Non-hostile Intercourse between Belligerents

Flags of Truce.

88. Non-hostile relations between belligerents must be conducted with scrupulous good faith. They are usually commenced by means of a flag of truce.

Non-hostile transactions between belligerents are technically described as " belli commercia ", a term which is similarly employed by Virgil, *Aeneid* x. 532, and by Tacitus, *Ann.* xiv. 33, *Hist.* ii. 81.

89. An individual is considered as being the bearer of a flag of truce who is authorized by one of the belligerents to enter into communication with the other, and who comes with a white flag. He has a right to inviolability, as have also the trumpeter, bugler, or drummer, the flag-bearer, and the interpreter, who may accompany him. (H. R. 32.)

The bearer of a flag of truce will, of course, enjoy the privileges of such, although he may come unaccompanied.

90. The Commander to whom a bearer of a flag of truce is sent is not obliged to receive him under all circumstances.

He can take all steps necessary to prevent the bearer of a flag of truce from taking advantage of his mission to obtain information.

In case of abuse, he has the right to detain the envoy temporarily. (H. R. 33.)

A Commander may, for instance, refuse to receive a flag of truce, or may direct the bearer to be blindfolded, if he is executing a secret movement. He may also, under certain circumstances, declare beforehand that a flag of truce cannot be received.

91. The bearer of a flag of truce loses his rights of inviolability if it is established, positively and beyond all question, that he has taken advantage of his privileged position to instigate or commit an act of treachery. (H. R. 34.)

" Trahison " in the original, i. e. " treason ", an offence of which, in strictness, an enemy cannot be guilty. " Trahison," and its German equivalent " Verrath ", or more specifically "Kriegsverrath", are, however, habitually employed in a much wider sense, as applicable to any acts on the part of inhabitants of invaded territory which are calculated either to deceive the invader, or to inform their own side of his forces and movements. See, e. g., the French *Code de Justice militaire*, and the *Kriegsbrauch* of the Prussian General Staff, p. 50.

Capitulations.

92. Capitulations agreed on between the Contracting Parties must be in accordance with the rules of military honour.

When once settled, they must be scrupulously observed by both the parties. (H. R. 35.)

A capitulation is an agreement for the surrender of troops or places.

A capitulation clearly in excess of the implied authority of the officer by whom it is made, when it is technically described as a mere "sponsion", as, for instance, that his troops shall never serve again against the same enemy, may be repudiated by his Government.

It is an implied condition, in the capitulation of a place, that the capitulating force shall not destroy its fortifications or stores, after the conclusion of the agreement.

Truces, Armistices, or Suspensions of Arms.

93. An armistice suspends military operations by mutual agreement between the belligerent parties. If its duration is not fixed, the belligerent parties can resume operations at any moment, provided always that previous notice, of such length as has been agreed upon, has been given to the enemy, in accordance with the terms of the armistice. (H. R. 36.)

There is no difference of meaning, according to British usage at least, between a "truce", an "armistice", and a "suspension of arms". See General Horsford's remarks at the Brussels Conference, *Parl. Paper*, Miscell. No. 1, 1875, p. 32.

94. An armistice may be general or local. The former suspends everywhere the military operations of the belligerent States; the latter, only those between certain fractions of the belligerent armies and within a fixed radius. (H. R. 37.)

A general armistice is, of course, in excess of the implied authority of a local Commander.

An armistice should specify, as far as possible, the acts which are forbidden, and those which are permitted, to the belligerents during its continuance.

95. An armistice must be notified officially, and in good time, to the proper authorities and to the troops. Hostilities are suspended immediately after the notification, or at the moment agreed upon. (H. R. 38.)

96. It is for the Contracting Parties to settle, in the terms of the armistice, what relations may be had by them, within the theatre of war, with the population and with each other. (H. R. 39.)

97. Any serious violation of the armistice by one of the parties gives the other party the right to denounce it, and even, in case of urgency, to recommence hostilities at once. (H. R. 40.)

98. A violation of the terms of the armistice, by individuals taking action on their own account, only confers a right to demand the punishment of the offenders, and compensation for any losses which may have been sustained. (H. R. 41.)

99. A treaty of peace, after signature, but before ratification, operates as a general armistice.

It is often desirable to interpose, during an armistice, a neutral zone between the belligerent forces.

Cartels.

100. The term "cartel" is most commonly employed to denote an arrangement entered into between the belligerents with reference to the exchange, or treatment, of prisoners. This term is, however, of general application, and may be used with reference to agreements for other purposes.

Cartels, as to prisoners, for other purposes.

Safe-conducts, Safe-guards, &c.

101. A belligerent often grants to enemy individuals a "passport", enabling them to pass unmolested through districts occupied by his forces. A "safe-conduct" has the same effect, but is applicable also to the carriage of goods, as is a "licence".

Passports. Safe-conducts. Licences.

A "safe-guard" is a notification by a belligerent Commander that buildings or other property upon which the notification is usually posted up, are exempt from interference on the

Safe-guards.

part of his troops. The term is also used to describe a guard, placed by the Commander to ensure such exemption. "Forcing a safe-guard" is a serious offence.

Cf. the Army Act, s. 6 (*c*).

SECTION IX

Authority in Occupied Territory *

Definition of Occupation.

Occupation defined.

102. Territory is considered to be occupied when it is placed as a matter of fact under the authority of the hostile army.

The occupation extends only to territories where that authority is established and capable of being exercised. (H. R. 42.)

The authority of the occupant may be exercised, by flying columns, beyond the places in which his forces are actually present, or in which the inhabitants have been disarmed.

The occupation of a given district should be, as far as possible, made known to the inhabitants of it, by proclamations posted up at the principal localities, or otherwise. But see Art. 12, *supra*.

It should be noted that all restrictions imposed upon an occupant apply, and with greater force, also to an invader of territory who is not yet in occupation of it.

The Position of the Occupant.

Occupant must maintain law and order.

103. The authority of the legitimate power having passed as a matter of fact into the hands of the occupant, he shall take all steps in his power to re-establish and ensure, so far as possible, public order and safety, while respecting, unless absolutely prevented, the laws in force in the country. (H. R. 43.)

* It will be obvious that many of the provisions of this Section would seem suitable for application also in non-occupied territory. Cf. *supra*, p. 5.

It may be necessary to vary the criminal, administrative, and other branches of Public Law, but hardly to interfere with the rules of Private Law, e.g. as to property, contracts, or family relations.

The occupant will often be glad to avail himself of the services of the native local authorities, so far as he can trust them, in case, and so long as, they are willing to continue in office.

In addition to so much of the native law as he considers suitable to be enforced, the occupant will also administer "martial law"; as to which see Arts. 4–13, *supra*.

Rights over Persons and Property.

[104. Any compulsion by a belligerent on the population of occupied territory to give information as to the army of the other belligerent, or as to his means of defence, is prohibited. (H. R. 44.)] He must not compel inhabitants to give information,

Does the prohibition here extend to compelling service as guides? The insertion of express words to that effect was opposed by Germany, Austria, Russia, and Japan. It was said that service as guides would be included in the phrase "operations of war", compulsion to take part in which is prohibited by H. R. 23, *last par.* (Art. 77, *supra*). But see the comment on that article. The German *Weissbuch*, p. 7, charges this article with selecting, in an undesirable way, single instances from the cases to which the principle contained in H. R. 23, *last par.*, is applicable; and so many other first-class Powers were opposed to the article that it is here included in square brackets.

105. Any compulsion on the population of occupied territory to take the oath to the hostile Power is prohibited. (H. R. 45.) or to take oath of allegiance.

A mere occupant has no right to exact an oath of allegiance from the population. He may, however, make such privileges as he may grant to them conditional upon their oath or promise not to take up arms against him, or to otherwise assist the enemy. This is sometimes described as an "oath of neutrality". For the form of oath sanctioned by Lord Roberts for this purpose in the Boer War, see *Parliamentary Paper* [Cd. 426] of 1900, p. 23.

Must respect lives, property, &c.

106. Family honour and rights, the lives of individuals, and private property, as also religious beliefs and liberty of public worship, must be respected.

Private property cannot be confiscated. (H. R. 46.)

Cf. Art. 15, *supra*, and the Army Act, s. 6 (1) (*f*), s. 49 (1).

Much controversy has been carried on as to the legitimacy of placing civilian inhabitants of occupied territory upon railway trains carrying troops of the invader, in order to prevent such trains from being fired upon. This was done by the Germans in France, in the war of 1870, and again by the British in the Boer War.

All that is said as to private property must, of course, be read subject to military necessity (see *supra*, p. 13), and, in particular, to Arts. 109–114, *infra*.

Pillage.

107. Pillage is formally prohibited. (H. R. 47.)

Pillage, or loot, was defined by General de Leer, at the Brussels Conference of 1874, as "booty which is not permitted"; and Baron Jomini explained that "there is a booty which is permissible on the field of battle—horses, &c. It is booty acquired at the expense of private property that the Commission means to prohibit", *Parl. Paper*, Miscell. No. 1, 1875, p. 128. Under the Army Prize-Money Act, 1832, British troops are to have such right and interest in booty as H.M. shall order.

Cf. Art. 83, *supra*, and the Army Act, s. 6 (1) (*a*), (*f*), (*g*), s. 49 (1).

Taxes, &c.

Taxes.

108. If, in the territory occupied, the occupant collects the taxes, dues and tolls, imposed for the benefit of the State, he shall do it, as far as possible, in accordance with the rules for assessment and incidence which are in force, and will in consequence be bound to defray the expenses of the administration of the occupied territory, to the extent to which the legitimate Government was bound to do so. (H. R. 48.)

Taxes, &c., imposed by the State, are here distinguished from rates, &c., imposed by local authorities.

Contributions.

109. If, besides the taxes contemplated in the preceding article, the occupant levies other money contributions in the occupied territory, this can only be for the needs of the army, or of the administration of such territory. (H. R. 49.) Contributions.

The occupant is not to levy contributions for the mere purpose of enriching himself.

It may sometimes be justifiable to levy a money contribution on one place, in order to spend it on the purchase of requisitions in kind at another place. The burden of the war may thus be more equitably distributed, falling on the inhabitants generally, rather than upon individual owners of the property which may be required.

110. No general penalty, pecuniary or otherwise, can be inflicted on the population on account of isolated acts for which it cannot be regarded as collectively responsible. (H. R. 50.) Penalties.

This article does not prejudge the question of Reprisals, as to which see Arts. 119, 120, *infra.*

111. No contribution shall be levied except under a written order, and on the responsibility of a Commander-in-chief. Contributions, how to be levied.

This levy shall, as far as possible, take place only in accordance with the rules which are in force for the assessment and incidence of taxes.

For every contribution a receipt shall be given to the payer. (H. R. 51.)

The "receipt" mentioned in this article is intended as evidence that money, goods, or services have been exacted, but implies, in itself, no promise to pay on the part of the occupant. He does not even thereby bind his Government, if victorious, to stipulate in the Treaty of Peace that the receipts shall be honoured by the Government of the territory which has been under occupation. A Swiss proposal, making it obligatory to honour the receipts mentioned in this and the following article, was indeed deliberately rejected at the first Hague Conference.

An occupant may, of course, incur a greater liability by the form which he chooses to give to his receipts, or under the terms of a general proclamation which he has issued.

Requisitions.

Requisitions.

112. Neither requisitions in kind, nor services, can be demanded from localities or inhabitants except for the needs of the army of occupation. They must be in proportion to the resources of the country, and of such a nature as not to imply any obligation upon the population to take part in operations of war against their country.

These requisitions and services shall only be demanded on the authority of the Commander in the locality occupied.

Supplies in kind shall, as far as possible, be paid for on the spot; if not, the fact that they have been taken shall be established by receipts, and the payment of the sums due shall be made as soon as possible. (H. R. 52.)

"Requisitions in kind" may, of course, relate not only to provisions, but also to horses, vehicles, clothing, tobacco, &c. The "services" here intended are such as would be rendered by drivers, blacksmiths, and artisans and labourers of all kinds; as also by the occupiers of houses upon which troops are quartered.

The phrase "for the needs of the army of occupation" was adopted rather than "for the necessities of the war", as being more favourable to the inhabitants.

The rules as to assessment, mentioned in Arts. 108, 111, *supra*, are obviously inapplicable to "requisitions" and "services", which can therefore be limited only by "the resources of the country".

The "operations of war" here intended would probably not comprise works at a distance from the scene of hostilities. Cf. Art. 77, *supra*.

"Requisitions" and "services" must obviously often be necessary when there is no time for reference to a higher authority than the Commander on the spot, or even for obtaining his order in writing.

Payment for supplies is even politic, as decreasing the chances of their being concealed. The provision that the receipts here mentioned shall be honoured by the belligerent on whose behalf they are signed was not contained in Art. 52 of the H. R. 1899.

On exacting contributions with a view to making payments for requisitions, see Art. 109, *comment, supra.*

Property, Public and Private.

113. An army of occupation can only take possession of cash, funds, and realizable securities, which are strictly State property, dépôts of arms, means of transport, stores and supplies, and generally all movable property of the State of a nature to be of use for operations of war. What State property may be appropriated.

All means employed on land, at sea, or in the air, for sending messages, for the carriage of persons or things, apart from cases governed by maritime law, dépôts of arms, and generally, all kinds of war material, may be taken possession of, even though belonging to private persons, but they must be restored, and the compensation to be paid for them shall be arranged for on the conclusion of peace. (H. R. 53.)

The first paragraph of this article is textually identical with Art. 6 of the Brussels *Projet* of 1874. For discussions as to its phraseology, see *Parl. Paper*, Miscell. No. 1, 1875, pp. 70, 138, 139.

It may be noted that considerable differences of opinion exist as to the meaning of the purposely ambiguous term, "Valeurs exigibles," here translated "realizable securities". It has been officially translated into German by "eintreibbare Forderungen".

The occupying army may not only "take possession" (*saisir*) of the things mentioned, but may also confiscate them for the benefit of its own Government absolutely. It must, however, be observed that some forms of property, nominally belonging to the State, e. g. the funds of savings banks, may be in reality private property, under State management.

As to railway plant which is neutral property, and has come from neutral territory, see *infra*, Art. 139 (H. v. 19).

Although no receipt is here required to be given, something of the sort is obviously desirable, with a view to subsequent compensation. The Treaty of Peace must settle upon whom the burden of making compensation is ultimately to fall.

Sub-marine cables.

114. Submarine cables, connecting a territory occupied with a neutral territory, shall not be seized or destroyed, unless in case of absolute necessity. They also must be restored, and the compensation to be paid for them shall be arranged for on the conclusion of peace. (H. R. 54.)

This new article, on a topic which the Conference of 1899 declined to discuss, with reference even to shore ends of cables, as not within its programme, takes the place occupied in the H. R. of that year by an article (54) relating to neutral railway material; as to which, see now *infra*, Art. 139 (H. v. 19).

When messages were first exchanged by Transatlantic cable between England and America in 1888, President Buchanan, in replying to a congratulatory despatch from Queen Victoria, inquired whether "all the nations of Christendom will not spontaneously unite in the declaration that *it shall be for ever neutral, and that its communications shall be held sacred in passing to the place of their destination, even in the midst of hostilities*". It need hardly be stated that the President's hope has not been realized. The International Convention for the Protection of Submarine Cables, signed at Paris on April 16, 1884, is expressly declared by its 15th article to "in no wise restrict the action of belligerents"; and H. R. 54, it will be observed, relates only to cables connecting neutral with occupied territories. The *Institut de Droit International*, in 1902, agreed upon five rules, by which it was thought that the treatment of cables by belligerents might reasonably be controlled, to the following effect: (1) a cable uniting two neutral territories is inviolable; (2) a cable uniting the territories of the two belligerents, or two localities in the territory of one of them, may be cut anywhere but in neutral waters; (3) a cable uniting the territories of a neutral and a belligerent may be cut only in the territorial waters of that belligerent, or in the High Seas within the limits of a blockade; (4) a neutral State must not permit messages clearly in the interest of one of the belligerents; (5) in the application of these rules, nothing is to turn on the cables being State or private, enemy or neutral, property (*Annuaire*, t. xix, p. 331). The rules of the *Institut* were substantially adopted in the United States Naval War Code of 1900 (revoked in 1904).

State lands,

115. The occupying State shall regard itself as being only administrator and usufructuary of the public buildings,

immovable property, forests and agricultural undertakings belonging to the hostile State, and situated in the occupied country. It must protect the substance of these properties, and administer them according to the rules of usufruct. (H. R. 55.) buildings, &c.

A person is said, in continental systems of law, to be a "usufructuary", or to enjoy a "usufruct", in property in which he has an interest of a special kind, for life or some lesser period. The "rules of usufruct" may be shortly stated to be that the property subject to the right must be so used that its substance sustains no injury.

Churches, schools, &c., and works of art, &c.

116. The property of localities (*communes*), as also that of institutions devoted to religion, charity, and education, and to the arts and sciences, even when State property, shall be treated as private property is treated.

All seizure, destruction, or intentional injury of such institutions, of historical monuments, or of works of art or science, is prohibited, and should be made the subject of proceedings. (H. R. 56.)

Under "property of localities" might come, e. g., town-halls, waterworks, gasworks, or police-stations.

This is now the last article of the Hague Regulations (as annexed in 1907 to H. iv). Neutral rights and duties, briefly dealt with in Arts. 57–60 of the Regulations of 1899, are now more fully defined in H. v (*infra*, Arts. 121–139).

SECTION X

Penalties for Violations of the Laws of War

Punishment of Offenders.

Punishment of actual offenders.

117. Individuals offending against the laws of war are liable to such punishment as is prescribed by the military code of the belligerent into whose hands they may fall, or, in default of such code, then to such punishment as may be ordered, in accordance with the laws and usages of war, by a military court.

118. When a whole corps systematically disregards the laws of war, e.g. by refusal of quarter, any individuals belonging to it, who are taken prisoners, may be treated as implicated in the offence.

At the Brussels Conference of 1874, a suggestion was made, on behalf of France, to provide by international agreement a single system for the repression of offences against the laws of war, to be put in force by each Power as part of its military law (*Parl. Paper*, Miscell. No. 1, 1875, p. 20). Nothing has, however, been done in this direction. With reference only to offences against the Geneva Convention, the *Institut de Droit International*, in 1895, drafted a set of rules (see *Annuaire*, t. xiv, p. 188); and the Geneva Convention of 1906 followed suit in Articles 27 and 28 (Arts. 68 and 69 *supra*), to which, as has already been explained, the British Government have been unable to accede. The unauthorized use of the Red Cross emblem had been, however, already made illegal in many countries, the laws of which upon this subject are set out in the *Actes de la Conférence*, pp. 166–174, as also in *Parl. Paper* 1908 [Cd. 3933], pp. 64–74. Very little is to be found in English Statutes or Regulations with reference to offences against International Law.

Reprisals.

Reprisals.

119. When the actual offenders cannot be reached or identified, resort is sometimes had to measures of "Reprisals" or "Retaliation", by which persons guilty of no offence may suffer for the acts of others. Since, however, the permissibility of such measures is a painful exception to the rule that a belligerent must observe the laws of war, even without reciprocity on the part of the enemy, Reprisals must be sparingly exercised, and then not by way of vengeance, but solely in order to prevent a repetition of the offence complained of.

Reprisals need not resemble in character the offence complained of. They may be exercised against persons or property. Only in extreme cases have prisoners of war been executed by way of reprisal; but the destruction of villages, houses, &c., on account of offences committed in them, or in their neighbourhood, has not been uncommon. Such destruction is not to be confused with that which is occasionally necessary for strategic reasons. Cf. *supra*, Arts. 3 and 76 (*g*).

120. Reprisals must be exercised only subject to the following restrictions:— Restrictions upon the practice.

1. The offence in question must have been carefully inquired into.

2. Redress for the wrong, or punishment of the real offender, must be unattainable.

3. The Reprisals must be authorized, unless under very special circumstances, by the Commander-in-chief.

4. They must not be disproportioned to the offence, and must in no case be of a barbarous character.

This article is intended to represent prevalent authoritative opinion upon this subject, as to which as yet no written rules have been adopted by international consent. The *Projet* of a Convention on the laws of war, submitted by Russia to the Brussels Conference of 1874, suggested the following articles:—69. "Reprisals are only admitted in extreme cases, regard being paid, as far as possible, to the laws of humanity, when it shall have been established beyond question that the laws and customs of war have been violated by the enemy, and that he has resorted to measures condemned by the Law of Nations." 70. "The choice of the means and the extent of reprisals should be proportioned to the gravity of the infraction of law perpetrated by the enemy. Reprisals which are disproportionately severe are contrary to the rules of the Law of Nations." 71. "Reprisals shall be allowed only on the authority of the Commander-in-chief, who must also determine the degree of their severity and their duration." (See *Parl. Paper*, Miscell. No. 1, 1874, p. 11.) The Conference, however, largely in deference to Belgian representations, declined to seem to add to the authority for a practice so repulsive, although, under certain circumstances, unavoidable, by legislating on the subject. The attempt to regulate the practice has not been renewed at the Hague Conferences of 1899 or 1907.

SECTION XI

The Rights and Duties of Neutral Powers and Individuals in case of War on Land*

The Rights and Duties of Neutral Powers.

Inviolability of neutral territory.

121. The territory of neutral Powers is inviolable. (H. v. 1.)

The territory of a neutral State, so long as the State fulfils its duties as neutral, must not be entered by troops of either belligerent, except for the purpose of asking to be interned therein.

Prohibition of belligerent passage;

122. Belligerents are forbidden to send across the territory of a neutral Power either troops, or convoys, whether of munitions of war or of provisions. (H. v. 2.)

N.B. that by Art. 125 *infra* (H. v. 5), it is the duty of the neutral Power to prevent belligerents from doing any of the acts which are prohibited by Arts. 122–124 (H. v. 2–4).

or radiographic instalment.

123. Belligerents are also forbidden:

(*a*) To install on the territory of a neutral Power a radio-telegraphic station, or any apparatus intended to serve as a means of communication with belligerent forces on land or at sea.

(*b*) To make use of any installation of that character, established by them before the war, on the territory of a neutral Power, and not previously open for forwarding public communications, for a purpose exclusively military. (H. v. 3.)

Clause (*a*) would prohibit such action as that of Russia in establishing a station on Chinese territory near Chefoo, by which communication was kept up between Port Arthur, while besieged, and the outer world.

In Clause (*b*), the insertion of the words "for a purpose exclusively

* The following 19 articles of Convention No. V of 1907 are in substitution for, and in amplification of, Arts. 57–60 of the Hague *Règlement* of 1899, as to the laws and customs of war on land.

military" was suggested by Russia, to meet objections raised by Great Britain and other Powers, with some reference to the International Radiographic Convention of 1906. Under Art. 125 (H. v. 5) *infra*, a neutral Power is bound to prevent such use as is prohibited by this clause.

124. Bodies of combatants cannot be formed, nor can recruiting offices be opened, in the interest of belligerents, on the territory of a neutral Power. (H. v. 4.)

Enlistments prohibited.

125. A neutral Power ought not to allow on its territory any of the acts contemplated by Articles 2 to 4.

It is under no obligation to punish acts in contravention of neutrality, unless those acts have been committed on its own territory. (H. v. 5.)

The neutral must prevent acts prohibited by Arts. 2–4.

A neutral State will, of course, not be expected to discharge the duties cast upon it by this article, and by Arts. 131–134 (H. v. 11–14) *infra*, should it be unprovided with forces sufficient to enable it to do so. Thus, at the Hague Conference of 1899, Luxemburg declared her inability to discharge such duties.

126. A neutral Power does not incur responsibility from the fact that individuals singly cross the frontier to enter the service of one of the belligerents. (H. v. 6.)

Acts for which a neutral is not responsible.

127. A neutral Power is not bound to prevent the exportation, or the passage, in the interest of one or other of the belligerents, of arms, munitions, or generally of everything which could be useful for an army or a fleet. (H. v. 7.)

This article, it will be observed, distinctly negatives the existence of any duty on the part of a neutral State to prevent the export from its territory of contraband of war. A school of writers, of whom M. Kleen may be taken as a leading representative (see his *De la Contrebande de guerre*, 1893, pp. 43–72), has endeavoured to impose this heavy burden upon neutral Governments, but without success. The *Institut de Droit International* was much occupied with the question from 1892 to 1906. See the *Annuaire*, tt. xiii, xiv, xv, xxi.

128. A neutral Power is not bound to forbid, or to prevent, the employment, for the belligerents, of telegraphic or telephonic cables, or of apparatus for wireless telegraphy, which are either its own property, or the property of companies or individuals. (H. v. 8.)

A neutral must act impartially.

129. All restrictive or prohibitive measures taken by a neutral Power, with reference to the matters dealt with in Articles 7 and 8, must be applied by it to the belligerents impartially.

The neutral Power shall see to this duty being respected by the companies or individuals owning telegraphic or telephonic cables, or apparatus for wireless telegraphy. (H. v. 9.)

Defence of neutrality is not hostility.

130. The fact that a neutral Power repels, even by force, intrusions upon its neutrality cannot be considered as a hostile act. (H. v. 10.)

*Belligerents interned, and wounded cared for, in neutral territory.**

Internment.

131. A neutral Power which receives in its territory troops belonging to belligerent armies shall intern them, as far as possible, at a distance from the theatre of war.

It may keep them in camps, and even confine them in fortresses or in places adapted for this purpose.

It will decide whether officers may be left at liberty on giving their parole that they will not leave the neutral territory without permission. (H. v. 11.)

The neutral Power may deport to another part of its dominions interned belligerent troops which cannot conveniently be kept in the territory in which they have sought refuge.

If a belligerent force, even accompanied by prisoners, enters

* Of the five articles which follow, four, viz. 131, 132, 134, 135 (H. v. 11, 12, 14, 15), were transferred textually in 1907 to this place from the Hague *Règlement* of 1899, where they figured as Arts. 57, 58, 59, 60. Art. 133 (H. v. 13) is new.

neutral territory in (proved) error, its immediate departure should be permitted.

132. In the absence of any special Convention, the neutral Power shall supply the interned with the food, clothing, and relief required by humanity.

Treatment of the interned;

At the conclusion of peace, the expenses caused by the internment shall be made good. (H. v. 12.)

Each belligerent will be responsible for the expenses caused by the internment of its own troops, in the absence of any treaty provision to the contrary.

133. A neutral Power which receives prisoners of war who have escaped shall leave them at liberty. If it permits them to remain on its territory, it may determine where they shall reside.

and of prisoners who have escaped or are brought in.

The same rule applies to prisoners of war brought with them by troops taking refuge in the territory of a neutral Power. (H. v. 13.)

134. A neutral Power may authorize the passage over its territory of wounded or sick belonging to the belligerent armies, on condition that the trains bringing them shall carry neither combatants nor war material. In such a case, the neutral Power is bound to adopt such measures of precaution and control as may be necessary for this purpose.

Passage of sick and wounded;

Wounded or sick who are brought, under these conditions, into neutral territory by one of the belligerents, and belong to the opposite party, must be detained by the neutral Power, so as to ensure their not taking part again in the operations of the war. The same duty shall devolve on the neutral Power with reference to wounded or sick of the other army who may be committed to its care. (H. v. 14.)

their internment.

The neutral Power, though it may do so, is not bound to allow such passage as is here mentioned. The privilege should be accorded impartially, if at all, nor should one belligerent be permitted to send his sick and wounded through the neutral territory without consent of the other belligerent, previously obtained.

Under the second paragraph, wounded prisoners, brought into neutral territory by a belligerent, may not be carried through as prisoners to the territory of their captor, but must remain under neutral control so long as the war lasts, when they will be allowed to return to their own country.

"The same duty," &c., i.e. of detaining wounded who, for some reason, are left in the neutral territory; instead of being merely carried through it, under the first paragraph of this article.

The Geneva Convention.

135. The Geneva Convention applies to sick and wounded interned in neutral territory. (H. v. 15.)

The regulative articles of the Geneva Convention of 1906 are set out as Arts. 42–69, *supra*.

Powers which do not ratify, or accede to, that Convention, but are parties to the Geneva Convention of 1864, remain bound by the earlier Convention, for the text of which, see *infra*, Appendix III, p. 135.

*Neutral Persons.**

Definition of neutrals.

[136. Those persons are considered to be neutrals who are subjects (*les nationaux*) of a State which takes no part in the war. (H. v. 16.)]

* The four articles which immediately follow, viz. 136–139 (H. v. 16–19), are the sole result of prolonged discussions in the Conference of 1907, upon a series of articles proposed by Germany, with the general support of Austria, Spain, and the United States, as to "the rights of neutrals in belligerent territory". The policy of Germany was to create for neutral persons and their property, so situated, an exceptionally favoured position, guaranteeing them against requisitions, and against liability, under any circumstances, to be called upon to take part in the defence of their temporarily adopted country. Belligerents were also to be expressly forbidden to accept offers of any "services de guerre" (a term which was to cover all assistance other than that of a religious or medical character) from neutrals; and a duty was to be thrown on neutral Governments of making it penal for their subjects to take service with either belligerent. Great Britain, France, Russia, and Japan successfully opposed this policy, and the bulk of the German articles failed, accordingly, to secure insertion. Cf. the *Weissbuch*, p. 8. Great Britain signed this Convention on June 29, 1908, under reserve of Arts. 16–18, which are accordingly enclosed in square brackets. The "Final Act" of 1907, it

Neutral subjects, taking part in hostilities on behalf of one belligerent, are liable to be treated by the other belligerent in every respect as if they were enemy subjects, and their own Government has no right to object to their being so treated. Neutrals aiding belligerents.

Neutral subjects resident in the territory of a belligerent are, equally with the other inhabitants of the country, liable to suffer in person and property through the events of the war; and their Governments acquire thereby no right to claim compensation on their behalf. Such compensation, if not awarded by the special provisions of a treaty, is given only as a matter of grace and favour. They are, for instance, liable to be removed from their homes, or even to be banished from the country, on suspicion of misconduct towards an occupying army, or for reasons of strategic convenience.

[137. A neutral cannot take advantage of his neutrality: Acts which forfeit,

(*a*) If he does acts of hostility against a belligerent.

(*b*) If he does acts in favour of a belligerent; especially if he voluntarily takes service in the ranks of the armed forces of one of the parties.

In such cases, the neutral shall not receive from the belligerent against whom he has departed from neutrality more rigorous treatment than might be received for the same act by a subject of the other belligerent State. (H.v.17.)]

It was agreed at the Conference of 1907 that expressions of sympathy are not "acts", within the meaning of Clause (*b*).

[138. The following acts shall not be considered to be acts done in favour of one of the belligerents within the meaning of Art. 17, letter *b* (*i.e.* Art. 137 (*b*) *supra*). acts which do not forfeit, neutral privileges.

(*a*) Furnishing goods, or making a loan, to one of the belligerents, provided that the person so furnishing, or lending, inhabits (*habite*) neither the territory of the other party, nor territory which is in the

may be observed, contains a *vœu* to the effect that "the Powers may settle, by special conventions, the situation, with reference to military requirements, of foreigners established in their territories".

occupation of that party, and that the goods furnished do not come from those territories.

(*b*) Rendering services in matters of police, or of civil administration. (H. v. 18.)]

Railway Material.

Neutral trains in belligerent territory.

139. Railway material coming from the territory of neutral Powers, whether belonging to those Powers, or to private companies or individuals, and capable of being identified as such, cannot be requisitioned or employed by a belligerent, unless in the case of, and to the extent required by, absolute necessity. It shall be sent back, as soon as possible, to the country to which it belongs.

Belligerent trains in neutral territory.

The neutral Power may similarly, in case of necessity, keep and employ, in the meantime, material belonging to the territory of the belligerent Power.

Compensation shall be paid, on either side, in proportion to the material employed and the duration of its employment. (H. v. 19.)

This article was suggested on behalf of Luxemburg, essentially a country of transit. It empowers, as will be observed, the neutral from whose territory the requisitioned railway plant has come, to supply its place for the time with railway plant which has come into its territory from that of the belligerent Power which authorized the requisition.

As to compensation, cf. Art. 114 (H. R. 54) *supra*.

Neutral property of other kinds.

140. Property of neutrals of other kinds, found in territory which is the scene of hostilities, even though not placed by them at the disposal of the enemy, is liable to be taken possession of, or even destroyed, for strategic reasons, by either belligerent; but compensation must in this case be made, by the belligerent so acting, to the neutral owners for the loss they have sustained.

APPENDICES

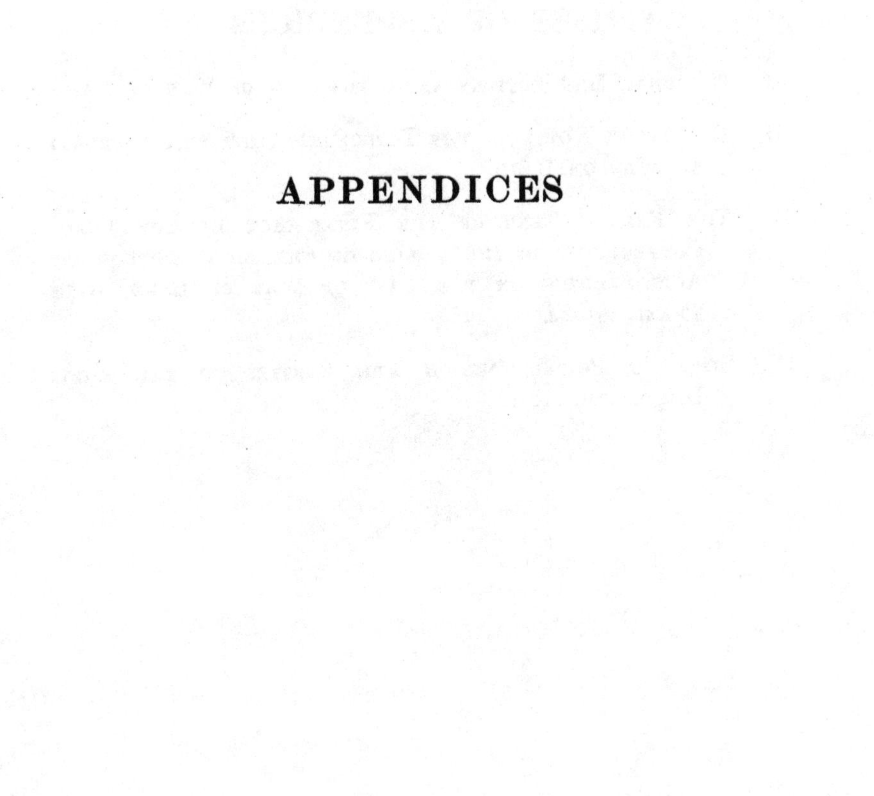

LIST OF APPENDICES

I. National Instructions as to the Law of War on Land.

II. Historical Notes on the Diplomatic Acts which relate to War on Land.

III. The French Text of the Final Act of the Peace Conference of 1907; also of the eight Diplomatic Acts bearing on the Law of War on Land, with Translations.

IV. Lists of Powers which are Parties to the eight Diplomatic Acts.

APPENDIX I

NATIONAL INSTRUCTIONS AS TO THE LAW OF WAR ON LAND

THE first Government to issue such instructions to its armies was that of the United States, during the civil war of 1861–1865.

The preparation of them was entrusted to Dr. Franz Lieber (b. 1800, d. 1872), who, after a stormy youth divided between legal study at several German Universities and military service, ending with a severe wound at the battle of Ligny, suffered imprisonment as politically dangerous, and found it expedient in 1825 to visit England, and two years later to settle in America. Here this remarkable man and prolific writer passed the rest of his life, for most of the time as Professor of History and Political Science, and later of International Law, first in South Carolina and then at Columbia College, New York. In the summer of 1862 he prepared for the United States Government an admirable report on guerrilla warfare, and in December of the same year was commissioned, with some military colleagues, to draw up a Code of Instructions for the government of armies in the field. The work was approved by the President, and issued to the army as General Order No. 100 of 1863. It was reissued in 1898.

The several sections deal with (1) Martial Law, military necessity, retaliation; (2) enemy property, protection of inhabitants; (3) prisoners, hostages, booty; (4) partisans, war-rebels; (5) spies, safe-conduct; (6) exchange of prisoners, flags of truce; (7) parole; (8) armistice; (9) assassination; (10) civil war. The Code is not well arranged, and its rules are in some respects more severe than those which would be enforced in a war between two independent States.

Lieber's estimate of the importance of his work may be gathered from the following extracts from letters written by him to General Halleck: "I have earnestly endeavoured to treat of these grave topics conscientiously and comprehensively; and you, well-read in the literature of international law, know that nothing of the kind exists in any language. I had no guide, no groundwork, no text-book. I can assure you that no counselor of Justinian sat down to his task of the Digest with a deeper feeling of the gravity of his labor than filled my breast in the laying down for the first time such a code, where nearly everything was floating. Usage, history, reason and conscientiousness, a sincere love of truth, justice, and civilization have been my guides; but of course the whole must still be very imperfect." "I think that No. 100 will do honour to our country. It will be adopted as basis for similar works by the English, French and Germans."

Lieber's expectation that the example of the United States would be followed in other countries has been but partially realized. Provisions bearing upon isolated topics of the international law of war no doubt occur incidentally, in such official documents as the French *Code de Justice militaire*, the Italian *Codice penale militare*, and the German *Felddienst-Ordnung*; but such systematic treatment of the subject as has been attempted, to the knowledge of the present writer, by national authority may be dismissed in a few paragraphs.

Prussia is known to have issued, at any rate as early as 1870, confidential instructions upon the subject for the guidance of officers. The Great General-staff, in 1902, issued the pamphlet entitled *Kriegsbrauch im Landkriege*, to which references have been made in the body of this work.

The Netherlands, in 1871, ordered that a practical manual upon the laws of war, drawn up by General den Beer Poortugael, should be used as a textbook in military schools.

France, in 1877, authorized for use in military schools a *Manuel de Droit International à l'usage des officiers de l'armée de terre*, prepared by M. Billot, which has since been kept up to date.

Russia, at the outset of the war of 1877 with Turkey, published in the official gazette a catechism setting forth, in simple language, the principles of the Geneva Convention, &c. &c., and in 1904 issued more elaborate *Instructions for the Russian Army respecting the Laws and Customs of War on Land.* (Translated for the British War Office [A. 495].)

SERVIA, in 1878, issued a manual for the use of officers.

THE ARGENTINE REPUBLIC, in 1881, adopted, for the instruction of its army, a Spanish edition of the *Manuel* of the Institut de Droit International.

SPAIN, in 1893, prescribed the use in military academies of a *Cartilla de leyes y usos de la guerra*, mainly founded upon a draft which had been adopted by a congress of officers, held at Madrid, representing the armies of Spain, Portugal, and the various Latin States of South and Central America.

GREAT BRITAIN, in the *Manual of Military Law*, first published by the War Office in 1883, has inserted a chapter on "the customs of war", compiled by the late Lord Thring from the ordinary textbooks on the subject. It was stated to have "no official authority", and to express "only the opinions of the compiler as drawn from the authorities cited". It was not till nearly twenty years later that the Secretary of State for War was induced to depart from this cautious attitude, and to entrust to the present writer the preparation of the *Handbook of the Laws and Customs of War on Land*, many thousand copies of which were issued by authority to the British Army in 1904.

The bare texts of Conventions and Declarations dealing with the laws of war may no doubt be found in the Government gazettes of most countries, as also in papers presented to their respective legislatures. They occur, for instance, in the "Treaty Series" of papers presented to the British Parliament; and may be discovered, though with more difficulty, for the period before 1892, when that series commences, in the larger series of "Parliamentary Papers: Diplomatic". In some countries these texts are also specially printed for army use, e.g. in the French *Bulletin Officiel du Ministère de la Guerre* and the Italian *Raccolta delle Convenzioni Internazionali che riguardano la Guerra*, issued by the Ministry of War.

APPENDIX II

HISTORICAL NOTES ON THE DIPLOMATIC ACTS WHICH RELATE TO WAR ON LAND

Several attempts have been made, since the middle of the nineteenth century, to systematize the laws of war by international discussion, and to procure the general acceptance of a uniform code of those laws by international agreement. These attempts have so far resulted, with reference to war on land, in the signature of eight diplomatically binding Acts.

The first topic to be thus dealt with was, in 1864, the treatment of the wounded. The choice of weapons engaged attention in 1868, and at length the Governments of the world took courage to deal with the conduct of warfare as a whole. Just before the close of the century, most of the civilized Powers entered into a Convention by which they bound themselves to promulgate to their respective armies instructions framed on one and the same comprehensive model. This Convention, signed at the first Peace Conference at the Hague, in 1899, and ratified in the following year by most of the Powers which had been represented at the Conference, incorporating, as it did, the Geneva Convention of 1864, as to the treatment of the wounded, and the St. Petersburg Declaration of 1868, as to explosive bullets, marked a considerable progress towards an International Code of the Law of War on land. The Conference of 1899, by large majorities, in which Great Britain was not included, supplemented the Convention by three Declarations as to prohibited methods of destruction.

The work of codifying the law on this subject was resumed in 1906, when a new Convention as to the treatment of the sick and wounded, to supersede that of 1864, was signed at a Conference which sat at Geneva from June 11 to July 6. In the following year the second Peace Conference, held at The Hague from June 15 to October 18, besides renewing No. 1 of the Hague Declarations of 1899, which had expired by lapse of time, framed three Conventions dealing with the law of war on land, viz. No. iii, relating to the opening of hostilities; No. iv, an amended reissue of the Convention of 1899 relating to the laws and customs of war on land; and No. v, relating to the rights and duties of neutral Powers and persons in case of war on land.

A short account of each of these International Acts will occupy the following pages.

(1.)

The Geneva Conventions (1864–1906).

The sufferings of the wounded in the Italian campaign of 1859, especially as made known by M. Henri Dunant's pamphlet, *Un Souvenir de Solférino* (1862), called attention to the urgent necessity for giving increased efficiency to the medical services of belligerents, and also for supplementing those services by organized voluntary effort, preparation for which must be made in time of peace. Thanks to the exertions of the "Société Genevoise d'Utilité Publique", an unofficial conference of persons of different nationalities, interested in the subject, was held at Geneva in 1863, which resolved to encourage the formation in each country of committees for the purpose of offering aid to the sanitary services of armies in the field. The agents of these "Sociétés de Secours" were to wear an armbadge (*brassard*), displaying a red cross on a white ground (the arms of the Swiss Confederation, transposing the colours). This was the origin of the so-called "Red Cross Societies", which have since rapidly multiplied under the guidance of the "Comité International", sitting at Geneva.

So far, what had been accomplished amounted merely to an organization of private philanthropic effort; but a suggestion made by the Conference of 1863 was destined to produce results of quite a different order.

The Swiss Government was induced to invite the Powers to a diplomatic Conference with a view to the "neutralization", by a permanent international agreement, of persons and appliances devoted to the relief of the sick and wounded in belligerent armies. A Conference assembled accordingly at Geneva, on Aug. 8, 1864, and produced a Convention (q. v. in Appendix III, *infra*, p. 135), which was signed on the 22nd of the same month by the representatives of twelve Powers, by all of which it was subsequently ratified. First and last, no fewer than fifty-four Powers became parties to this Convention,* the object of which was to give international protection in time of war to the wounded, as also to the hospitals and medical services of both sides alike. It is necessary to observe, because the fact has occasionally been lost sight of, that the Convention, though it adopted, for its own purposes, the red-cross emblem of the "Sociétés de Secours", made no mention of such voluntary societies, still less did it confer upon them any privileges, but referred exclusively to the plant and personnel of the sanitary (i. e. medical and surgical) services of the belligerent Powers.†

Some difficulties which had been experienced in the working of the Convention led to the following steps being taken towards its amendment.

In consequence of representations made by the Red Cross Societies assembled at Paris on the occasion of the Exhibition of 1867, a diplomatic Conference met at Geneva in the following year, upon the invitation of the Swiss Government, with a view to the revision of the Convention of 1864. The Conference, which was attended by representatives of Austria, Baden, Bavaria, Belgium, Denmark, France, Great Britain, Italy, the Netherlands, North Germany, Sweden and Norway, Switzerland, Turkey, and Würtemberg, lasted from October 5 to 20, and resulted in the adoption of certain "additional articles". These, though never ratified, produced some effect upon public opinion, and were adopted, as a *modus vivendi*, by the French and Germans in 1870, and by the United States and Spain in 1898.‡

In 1899 the delegates to the "Peace Conference" at The Hague unanimously agreed to the following *vœu*: "The Conference,

* For the list of parties, see Appendix IV, *infra*, p. 140. For the Protocols of this Conference, see *Nouveau Recueil Général*, t. xx, pp. 375–399.

† Cf. Art. 51 of the present work, *supra*, p. 31.

‡ For the text of these articles, see *Nouveau Recueil Général*, t. xviii, pp. 612–619; and for the Protocols of the Conference, *ib.*, t. xx, pp. 400–435.

having regard to the preliminary steps taken by the Federal Government of Switzerland for the revision of the Convention of Geneva, expresses its hope that a special Conference for the purpose of revising the Convention may be summoned at an early date."

The Federal Government accordingly, in 1901 and 1903, invited the Powers to send delegates to a Conference for this purpose, and the British delegates in the latter year proceeded to hold a series of meetings, and agreed upon a draft form of revised Convention, which influenced to a considerable extent the new Convention which was ultimately made.

After further postponements, partly due to the Russo-Japanese war, the Conference met at Geneva on June 11, 1906. It was attended by the representatives of thirty-five Powers, and on July 6 signed a Convention, in thirty-three articles, designed to supersede that of 1864.* It has been largely ratified. The British ratification, which does not extend to Arts. 23, 27, 28, as to which, see *supra*, pp. 38–40, took place on April 16, 1907. Signatories of the old Convention remain bound by it till they have ratified, or adhered to, the new one.†

(2.)

The Declaration of St. Petersburg (1868).

Standard writers of the eighteenth century objected to the employment of certain means of injuring the enemy, on account of their wholesale destructiveness. The tendency of modern opinion is, however, against the prohibition of a weapon because it is effective. Since the duration of a war must largely depend upon the number of men who are put *hors de combat*, it may well be thought that, even in the interests of humanity, the more rapidly that object is accomplished, the better.‡

* Arts. 1–28 (omitting 24) of this Convention appear as Arts. 41–69 of the present work.

† For the text of the Convention of 1906 see *infra*, Appendix III, p. 111, and for the parties to it, Appendix IV, p. 140. For the *Actes* of the Geneva Conference of 1906, see the admirably edited official volume, issued by the Swiss Government: Genève, 1906. Cf. *Parl. Paper* [Cd. 3933], 1908.

‡ The Hague Declaration against the employment of projectiles charged

On the other hand, it is generally felt that some of the inventions of modern science are calculated to cause suffering and mortality in excess of what is needed to disable troops for present military service. Only four inventions of the kind have yet been condemned by general international agreement.

In 1863 a bullet was introduced into the Russian army, to be used for blowing up ammunition wagons, which exploded, by means of a cap, on contact with a hard substance. The fear that this sort of bullet might be employed against troops was increased when, in 1867, a modification of it was suggested which enabled it to explode, without a cap, on contact even with a soft substance. The Russian War Minister, General Milutine, was reluctant, therefore, to sanction the use of the bullet, as thus modified, and induced his Government to issue a circular to the Powers, inviting them to send delegates to an "International Military Commission", for the consideration of the question which had arisen. The Prussian Government was disposed to enlarge the scope of the inquiry, so as to enable it to deal generally with the application of scientific discoveries to warfare. To this Great Britain was opposed, and her view was found to be shared by the other Powers when the delegates met at St. Petersburg on Oct. 29 (Nov. 9), 1868. They agreed upon a Declaration, prohibiting the employment of the bullets in question, on Nov. 4 (16th), and it was signed on behalf of the seventeen Powers concerned by their diplomatic representatives at the Russian Court, as Plenipotentiaries, on Nov. 29 (Dec. 11).* Brazil subsequently acceded to it.

This Declaration (see Articles 71 and 72 of the present work, *supra*, p. 41) is of great value for the possibly too sweeping statement of general principles which it contains, although the projectiles against the use of which it is directed would perhaps, in any case, no longer be employed.

It is one of the "special Conventions" to which reference is made in Art. 23 of the Hague Convention No. iv of 1907.

with deadly gases (q. v. Appendix III, p. 126, *infra*) might seem to indicate a reaction towards the older view on the part of its signatories.

* For the Protocols of the Commission, see *Nouveau Recueil Général*, t. xviii, pp. 450–473; for the Declaration, *ib.*, t. xx, pp. 474, 475, and *infra*, Appendix III, p. 121.

(3.)

The Hague Conventions concerning the Laws of War on Land (1899–1907).

The first attempt to methodize, and to express in the form of an international agreement, the whole topic of the laws and usages of war, was made by the Conference convened at Brussels in 1874 by the Emperor Alexander II of Russia. The Conference produced a draft Declaration, in fifty-six articles, which, though it remained unratified, yet, resulting as it did from the deliberations of highly qualified delegates of thirteen of the principal States of Europe, has largely contributed to the formation of opinion upon the subject of which it treats.*

When, after the lapse of a quarter of a century, the Emperor Nicholas II procured the assembling of the delegates of twenty-six Powers for the first "Peace Conference" at The Hague, one of the subjects suggested for its consideration was a revision of the Brussels draft. The Convention and annexed *Règlement*, by which this work was accomplished, signed at The Hague on July 29, 1899, or subsequently, on behalf of all but three of the Powers represented, and afterwards ratified by almost all the signatories, besides receiving the accessions of very many other Powers, was not the least important piece of work accomplished by the Conference. It gave international obligation to a body of rules which were, for the most part, those which had been adopted at Brussels in 1874, with modifications derived from various sources, and especially from the *Manuel des lois de la guerre sur terre*, adopted by the Institut de Droit International, at its meeting at Oxford in 1880.†

On Oct. 21, 1904, Mr. Hay, on behalf of President Roosevelt, circulated a suggestion for the assembling of a second "Peace

* See *Parl. Paper*, Miscell. No. 1, 1875.

† For the Protocols of the Hague Conference of 1899, see *Nouveau Recueil Général*, 2me Série, t. xxvi, also *Parl. Paper*, Miscell. No. 1, 1899. It may be worth while to remark that this Blue-book, and that mentioned in the preceding note, are so misarranged, by intermixture of covering letters and despatches to and from the Home Government, as vastly to increase the labour of consulting them. A great improvement is observable in the Blue-book, Miscell. No. 4, 1908, in which the Protocols of the Second Peace Conference are continuously set out in chronological order, uninterrupted by alien matter, and are preceded by an analytical table of contents.

Conference", but eventually ceded the initiative in the matter to Russia. The Emperor Nicholas II accordingly, on April 3, 1906, proposed that the Conference should meet at The Hague in the latter half of July in that year; at the same time communicating to the Powers a programme for its discussions, which after stating that "With reference to the regulation of the Laws and Customs of War on Land, the conclusions arrived at by the first Conference need to be so supplemented and defined as shall prevent any misunderstanding of them", goes on to suggest for consideration: "Additions to be made to the provisions of the Convention of 1899 concerning the Laws and Customs of War on Land; among others, concerning the opening of hostilities, the rights of neutrals on land, &c.; the Declarations of 1899: one of them having lapsed, the question of its renewal."

The revision of the Convention of 1899, which dealt with these topics, engaged, therefore, much of the attention of the second Conference, when, after several postponements, it at last met on June 15, 1907.

A new Convention concerning the Laws of War on Land was adopted on Aug. 17, and has been largely ratified. It is practically a re-publication of the old one, with some variations of no great importance, except that Arts. 57–60 of the originally annexed *Règlement* are now detached from it, in order to their insertion, with new matter, in a separate Convention, dealing with neutral rights and duties in time of war on land.

Arts. 1–56 of the *Règlement* of 1907 are set out as Arts. 21–41, 70, 76–84, 86, 87, 89–98, 102–116 of the present work.

(4, 5, 6.)

The Three Hague Declarations of 1899–1907.

The Final Act of the Hague Conference of 1899 set out three Declarations, of which the first, which prohibited throwing projectiles or explosives from balloons, having expired by efflux of the five years to which its duration was limited, was renewed "to the end of the Third Peace Conference", at the Conference of 1907, subject to denunciation by any Power, to take effect in one year, so far as that Power is concerned. The Second and Third Declarations, prohibiting respectively the employment of projectiles the sole object of which is the diffusion of asphyxiating or harmful gases, and of bullets which expand or flatten easily in the human body, were signed without limit of time, though similarly terminable by denunciation.

Great Britain was originally a party to none of these Declarations; but on Aug. 30, 1907, formally acceded to the Second and Third. On June 29, 1908, she signed the First Declaration, as re-drafted in 1907, although a minority which includes most of the Great Powers has refused to revive it.

All three Declarations have, however, now been accepted by the greater number of the Powers, and must be taken to be included, with the Declaration of St. Petersburg, in the "special Conventions" mentioned in Art. 23 of the Hague Convention of 1907, as prohibiting certain modes of warfare. On the defective authority of Declaration No. 1, see, however, the *comment* on Art. 73 of this work, *supra*, p. 41, and the list of dissidents in Appendix IV, *infra*, p. 141.

(7.)

The Hague Convention No. iii of 1907, concerning the Commencement of Hostilities.

The necessity for something amounting to a Declaration of War before the commencement of hostilities has been much discussed in recent times with reference to the outbreak of war between Russia and Japan; and, some years before that event, with reference to the objections urged by British military authorities to the construction of a Channel tunnel. See the Report, prepared for the War Office in 1883, by Lt.-Colonel (now Major-General) F. Maurice, upon *Hostilities without Declaration of War*; and cf. the Resolutions of the *Institut de Droit International*, voted at Ghent in 1906, *Annuaire*, t. xxi, p. 292. The topic was included in the Russian programme for the Peace Conference of 1907, which accordingly drew up a Convention, Arts. 1 and 2 of which figure as Arts. 16 and 17 of the present work. For the full text of the Convention see *infra*, Appendix III, pp. 92–96.

(8.)

The Hague Convention, No. v of 1907, concerning the Rights and Duties of Neutral Powers and Individuals in Case of War on Land.

The *Règlement* annexed to the Hague Convention concerning the laws and usages of war on land, as adopted in 1899, contained four articles (57–60) dealing with "belligerents interned, and wounded cared for, in neutral territory". These articles, as already mentioned, have been omitted from the *Règlement* as revised in 1907, but are now placed with other matter in a new Convention, purporting to deal with the whole topic of neutral rights and duties with reference to land warfare. The Convention consists of twenty-five articles, of which Arts. 1–19 figure as Arts. 121–139 of the present work. For the other articles, forming the diplomatic framework of the Convention, see *infra*, Appendix III, p. 129.

APPENDIX III

CONTAINING THE FRENCH TEXT OF THE FINAL ACT OF THE PEACE CONFERENCE OF 1907, AND OF THE CONVENTIONS AND DECLARATIONS ADOPTED OR CONFIRMED BY THE CONFERENCE, HAVING REFERENCE TO WAR ON LAND, VIZ.: CONVENTIONS NOS. iii AND iv OF 1907, THE GENEVA CONVENTION OF 1906, THE ST. PETERSBURG DECLARATION OF 1868, THE HAGUE DECLARATIONS OF 1899–1907, AND CONVENTION NO. V OF 1907.

Each of these Acts is followed by an English translation of such portions of it as have not been already set out in the continuously numbered articles of the present work. Since the Powers parties to the Geneva Convention of 1864, and to the Hague Convention as to the laws of war on land of 1899, remain bound by these Acts till they have accepted the Acts superseding them, it has been thought worth while to add to this Appendix the text of the old Geneva Convention, and a note on the differences between the Conventions of 1899 and of 1907 with reference to land warfare.

ACTE FINAL DE LA DEUXIÈME CONFÉRENCE INTERNATIONALE DE LA PAIX.

(October 18, 1907.)

La Deuxième Conférence Internationale de la Paix, proposée d'abord par Monsieur le Président des États-Unis d'Amérique, ayant été, sur l'invitation de Sa Majesté l'Empereur de Toutes les Russies, convoquée par Sa Majesté la Reine des Pays-Bas, s'est réunie le 15 juin 1907 à La Haye, dans la Salle des Chevaliers, avec la mission de donner un développement nouveau aux principes humanitaires qui ont servi de base à l'œuvre de la Première Conférence de 1899.

Les Puissances, dont l'énumération suit, ont pris part à la Conférence, pour laquelle Elles avaient désigné les Délégués nommés ci-après : *

L'Allemagne, Les États-Unis d'Amérique, La République Argentine, L'Autriche-Hongrie, La Belgique, La Bolivie, Le Brésil, La Bulgarie, Le Chili, La Chine, La Colombie, La République de Cuba, Le Danemark, La République Dominicaine, La République de l'Équateur, L'Espagne, La France.

La Grande-Bretagne.—Son Exc. The Right Honourable Sir Edward Fry, G.C.B., Membre du Conseil Privé, Ambassadeur Extraordinaire, Membre de la Cour Permanente d'Arbitrage, Délégué Plénipotentiaire; Son Exc. The Right Honourable Sir Ernest Mason Satow, G.C.M.G., Membre du Conseil Privé, Membre de la Cour Permanente d'Arbitrage, Délégué Plénipotentiaire; Son Exc. The Right Honourable Lord Reay, G.C.S.I., G.C.I.E., Membre du Conseil Privé, Ancien Président de l'Institut de Droit International, Délégué Plénipotentiaire; Son Exc. Sir Henry Howard, K.C.M.G., C.B., Envoyé Extraordinaire et Ministre Plénipotentiaire à La Haye, Délégué Plénipotentiaire; M. le Général de Division Sir Edmond R. Elles, G.C.I.E., K.C.B., Délégué militaire; M. le Capitaine de vaisseau C. L. Ottley, M.V.O., R.N., A.D.C., Délégué naval; M. Eyre Crowe, Conseiller d'Ambassade, Délégué technique, Premier Secrétaire de la Délégation; M. Cecil Hurst, Conseiller d'Ambassade, Délégué technique, Conseiller légal de la Delégation; M. le Lieutenant-Colonel, The Honourable Henry Yarde-Buller, D.S.O., Attaché militaire à La Haye, Délégué technique; M. le Capitaine de frégate J. R. Segrave, R.N., Délégué technique; M. le Commandant George K. Cockerill, Chef de Section à l'État-Major de l'Armée, Délégué technique.

La Grèce, Le Guatémala, La République d'Haïti, L'Italie, Le Japon, Le Luxembourg, Le Mexique, Le Monténégro, Le Nicaragua, La Norvège, Le Panama, Le Paraguay, Les Pays Bas, Le Pérou,

* It has not been thought necessary to print here the names of Delegates of States other than Great Britain. They are set out in *Parl. Paper*, Miscell. No. 1 (1908).

*La Perse, Le Portugal, La Romanie, La Russie, Le Salvador, La Serbie, Le Siam, La Suède, La Suisse, La Turquie, L'Uruguay, Les États-Unis du Venezuela.**

Dans une série de réunions, tenues du 15 juin au 18 octobre 1907, où les Délégués précités ont été constamment animés du désir de réaliser, dans la plus large mesure possible, les vues généreuses de l'Auguste Initiateur de la Conférence et les intentions de leurs Gouvernements, la Conférence a arrêté, pour être soumis à la signature des Plénipotentiaires, le texte des Conventions et de la Déclaration énumérées ci-après et annexées au présent Acte :

I. Convention pour le règlement pacifique des conflits internationaux.

II. Convention concernant la limitation de l'emploi de la force pour le recouvrement de dettes contractuelles.

III. Convention relative à l'ouverture des hostilités.

IV. Convention concernant les lois et coutumes de la guerre sur terre.

V. Convention concernant les droits et les devoirs des Puissances et des personnes neutres en cas de guerre sur terre.

VI. Convention relative au régime des navires de commerce ennemis au début des hostilités.

VII. Convention relative à la transformation des navires de commerce en bâtiments de guerre.

VIII. Convention relative à la pose de mines sous-marines automatiques de contact.

IX. Convention concernant le bombardement par des forces navales en temps de guerre.

X. Convention pour l'adaptation à la guerre maritime des principes de la Convention de Genève.

XI. Convention relative à certaines restrictions à l'exercice du droit de capture dans la guerre maritime.

XII. Convention relative à l'établissement d'une Cour internationale des prises.

XIII. Convention concernant les droits et les devoirs des Puissances neutres en cas de guerre maritime.

* Forty-seven States were invited to the Conference. Of these Costa Rica and Honduras took no part in it. Corea was not separately represented.

XIV. Déclaration relative à l'interdiction de lancer des projectiles et des explosifs du haut de ballons.

Ces Conventions et cette Déclaration formeront autant d'actes séparés. Ces actes porteront la date de ce jour et pourront être signés jusqu'au 30 juin 1908 à La Haye par les Plénipotentiaires des Puissances représentées à la Deuxième Conférence de la Paix.

La Conférence, se conformant à l'esprit d'entente et de concessions réciproques qui est l'esprit même de ses délibérations, a arrêté la Déclaration suivante qui, tout en réservant à chacune des Puissances représentées le bénéfice de ses votes, leur permet à toutes d'affirmer les principes qu'Elles considèrent comme unanimement reconnus:

Elle est unanime,

1° A reconnaître le principe de l'arbitrage obligatoire;

2° A déclarer que certains différends, et notamment ceux relatifs à l'interprétation et à l'application des stipulations conventionnelles internationales, sont susceptibles d'être soumis à l'arbitrage obligatoire sans aucune restriction.

Elle est unanime enfin à proclamer que, s'il n'a pas été donné de conclure dès maintenant une Convention en ce sens, les divergences d'opinion qui se sont manifestées n'ont pas dépassé les limites d'une controverse juridique, et qu'en travaillant ici ensemble pendant quatre mois, toutes les Puissances du monde, non seulement ont appris à se comprendre et à se rapprocher davantage, mais ont su dégager, au cours de cette longue collaboration, un sentiment très élevé du bien commun de l'humanité.

En outre, la Conférence a adopté à l'unanimité la Résolution suivante :

La Deuxième Conférence de la Paix confirme la Résolution adoptée par la Conférence de 1899 à l'égard de la limitation des charges militaires; et, vu que les charges militaires se sont considérablement accrues dans presque tous les pays depuis ladite année, la Conférence déclare qu'il est hautement désirable de voir les Gouvernements reprendre l'étude sérieuse de cette question.

Elle a, de plus, émis les Vœux suivants :

1° La Conférence recommande aux Puissances signataires l'adoption du projet ci-annexé de Convention pour l'établissement d'une Cour de Justice arbitrale, et sa mise en vigueur dès qu'un accord sera intervenu sur le choix des juges et la constitution de la Cour.

2° La Conférence émet le vœu qu'en cas de guerre, les Autorités compétentes, civiles et militaires, se fassent un devoir tout spécial d'assurer et de protéger le maintien des rapports pacifiques et notamment des relations commerciales et industrielles entre les populations des États belligérants et les Pays neutres.

3° La Conférence émet le vœu que les Puissances règlent, par des Conventions particulières, la situation, au point de vue de charges militaires, des étrangers établis sur leurs territoires.

4° La Conférence émet le vœu que l'élaboration d'un règlement relatif aux lois et coutumes de la guerre maritime figure au programme de la prochaine Conférence et que, dans tous les cas, les Puissances appliquent, autant que possible, à la guerre sur mer, les principes de la Convention relative aux lois et coutumes de la guerre sur terre.

Enfin, la Conférence recommande aux Puissances la réunion d'une troisième Conférence de la Paix qui pourrait avoir lieu, dans une période analogue à celle qui s'est écoulée depuis la précédente Conférence, à une date à fixer d'un commun accord entre les Puissances, et elle appelle leur attention sur la nécessité de préparer les travaux de cette troisième Conférence assez longtemps à l'avance pour que ses délibérations se poursuivent avec l'autorité et la rapidité indispensables.

Pour atteindre à ce but, la Conférence estime qu'il serait très désirable que, environ deux ans avant l'époque probable de la réunion, un Comité préparatoire fût chargé par les Gouvernements de recueillir les diverses propositions à soumettre à la Conférence, de rechercher les matières susceptibles d'un prochain Règlement international et de préparer un programme que les Gouvernements arrêteraient assez tôt pour qu'il pût être sérieusement étudié dans chaque pays. Ce Comité serait, en outre, chargé de proposer un mode d'organisation et procédure pour la Conférence elle-même.

En foi de quoi, les Plénipotentiaires ont signé le présent Acte et y ont apposé leurs cachets.

Fait à La Haye, le dix-huit octobre mil neuf cent sept, en un seul exemplaire qui sera déposé dans les archives du Gouvernement des Pays-Bas, et dont des copies, certifiées conformes, seront délivrées à toutes les Puissances représentées à la Conférence.

TRANSLATION.

FINAL ACT OF THE SECOND INTERNATIONAL PEACE CONFERENCE.

(October 18, 1907.)

The Second International Peace Conference, proposed in the first instance by the President of the United States of America, having been convoked, on the invitation of His Majesty the Emperor of All the Russias, by Her Majesty the Queen of the Netherlands, assembled on the 15th June, 1907, at The Hague, in the Hall of the Knights, for the purpose of giving a fresh development to the humanitarian principles which served as a basis for the work of the First Conference of 1899.

The following Powers took part in the Conference, and appointed the Delegates named below:—

(*See supra*, p. 84.)

Great Britain:

His Excellency the Right Honourable Sir Edward Fry, G.C.B., Member of the Privy Council, Ambassador Extraordinary, Member of the Permanent Court of Arbitration, Delegate Plenipotentiary;

His Excellency the Right Honourable Sir Ernest Mason Satow, G.C.M.G., Member of the Privy Council, Member of the Permanent Court of Arbitration, Delegate Plenipotentiary;

His Excellency the Right Honourable Lord Reay, G.C.S.I., G.C.I.E., Member of the Privy Council, ex-President of the Institute of International Law, Delegate Plenipotentiary;

His Excellency Sir Henry Howard, K.C.M.G., C.B., Envoy Extraordinary and Minister Plenipotentiary at The Hague, Delegate Plenipotentiary;

Lieutenant-General Sir Edmond R. Elles, G.C.I.E., K.C.B., Military Delegate;

Captain C. L. Ottley, M.V.O., R.N., A.D.C., Naval Delegate;

Mr. Eyre Crowe, Councillor of Embassy, Technical Delegate, First Secretary to the delegation;

Mr. Cecil Hurst, Councillor of Embassy, Technical Delegate, Legal Adviser to the delegation;

Lieutenant-Colonel the Honourable Henry Yarde-Buller, D.S.O., Military Attaché at The Hague, Technical Delegate;

Commander J. R. Segrave, R.N., Technical Delegate;

Major George K. Cockerill, General Staff, Technical Delegate.

At a series of meetings, held from the 15th June to the 18th October, 1907, in which the above Delegates were throughout animated by the desire to realize, in the fullest possible measure, the generous views of the august initiator of the Conference and the intentions of their Governments, the Conference drew up for submission for signature by the Plenipotentiaries, the text of the Conventions and of the Declaration enumerated below and annexed to the present Act:—

1. Convention for the Pacific Settlement of International Disputes.

2. Convention respecting the Limitation of the Employment of Force for the Recovery of Contract Debts.

3. Convention relative to the Opening of Hostilities.

4. Convention respecting the Laws and Customs of War on Land.

5. Convention respecting the Rights and Duties of Neutral Powers and Persons in case of War on Land.

6. Convention relative to the Status of Enemy Merchant-ships at the outbreak of Hostilities.

7. Convention relative to the Conversion of Merchant-ships into War-ships.

8. Convention relative to the Laying of Automatic Submarine Contact Mines.

9. Convention respecting Bombardment by Naval Forces in Time of War.

10. Convention for the Adaptation to Naval War of the Principles of the Geneva Convention.

11. Convention relative to certain Restrictions with regard to the Exercise of the Right of Capture in Naval War.

12. Convention relative to the creation of an International Prize Court.

13. Convention concerning the Rights and Duties of Neutral Powers in Naval War.

14. Declaration prohibiting the discharge of Projectiles and Explosives from Balloons.

These Conventions and Declaration shall form so many separate Acts. These Acts shall be dated this day, and may be signed up to the 30th June, 1908, at The Hague, by the Plenipotentiaries of the Powers represented at the Second Peace Conference.

The Conference, actuated by the spirit of mutual agreement and concession characterizing its deliberations, has agreed upon the following Declaration, which, while reserving to each of the Powers represented full liberty of action as regards voting, enables them to affirm the principles which they regard as unanimously admitted:—

It is unanimous—

1. In admitting the principle of compulsory arbitration.

2. In declaring that certain disputes, in particular those relating to the interpretation and application of the provisions of International Agreements, may be submitted to compulsory arbitration without any restriction.

Finally, it is unanimous in proclaiming that, although it has not yet been found feasible to conclude a Convention in this sense, nevertheless the divergences of opinion which have come to light have not exceeded the bounds of judicial controversy, and that, by working together here during the past four months, the collected Powers not only have learnt to understand one another and to draw closer together, but have succeeded in the course of this long collaboration in evolving a very lofty conception of the common welfare of humanity.

The Conference has further unanimously adopted the following Resolution:—

The Second Peace Conference confirms the Resolution adopted by the Conference of 1899 in regard to the limitation of military expenditure; and inasmuch as military expenditure has considerably increased in almost every country since that time, the Conference declares that it is eminently desirable that the Governments should resume the serious examination of this question.

It has besides expressed the following wishes (*vœux*):—

1. The Conference calls the attention of the Signatory Powers to the advisability of adopting the annexed draft Convention for the creation of a Judicial Arbitration Court, and of bringing it into force as soon as an agreement has been reached respecting the selection of the Judges and the constitution of the Court.

2. The Conference expresses the wish that, in case of war, the responsible authorities, civil as well as military, should make it their special duty to ensure and safeguard the maintenance of pacific relations, more especially of the commercial and industrial relations

between the inhabitants of the belligerent States and neutral countries.

3. The Conference expresses the wish that the Powers should regulate, by special Treaties, the position, as regards military charges, of foreigners residing within their territories.

4. The Conference expresses the wish that the preparation of regulations relative to the laws and customs of naval war should figure in the programme of the next Conference, and that in any case the Powers may apply, as far as possible, to war by sea the principles of the Convention relative to the Laws and Customs of War on Land.

Finally, the Conference recommends to the Powers the meeting of a Third Peace Conference, which might be held within a period corresponding to that which has elapsed since the preceding Conference, at a date to be fixed by common agreement between the Powers, and it calls their attention to the necessity of preparing the programme of this Third Conference a sufficient time in advance to ensure its deliberations being conducted with the necessary authority and expedition.

In order to attain this object the Conference considers that it would be very desirable that, some two years before the probable date of the meeting, a preparatory Committee should be charged by the Governments with the task of collecting the various proposals to be submitted to the Conference, of ascertaining what subjects are ripe for embodiment in an International Regulation, and of preparing a programme which the Governments should decide upon in sufficient time to enable it to be carefully examined by the countries interested. This Committee should further be entrusted with the task of proposing a system of organization and procedure for the Conference itself.

In faith whereof the Plenipotentiaries have signed the present Act and have affixed their seals thereto.

Done at The Hague, the 18th October, 1907, in a single copy, which shall remain deposited in the archives of the Government of the Netherlands, and copies of which certified as correct shall be sent to all the Powers represented at the Conference.

CONVENTION No. iii.

RELATIVE A L'OUVERTURE DES HOSTILITÉS.

Sa majesté le Roi du Royaume-Uni de Grande Bretagne et d'Irlande, &c.

(*The list of Powers is the same as in the Acte Final, supra, p.* 84.)

Considérant que, pour la sécurité des relations pacifiques, il importe que les hostilités ne commencent pas sans un avertissement préalable;

Qu'il importe, de même, que l'état de guerre soit notifié sans retard aux Puissances neutres;

Désirant conclure une Convention à cet effet, ont nommé pour Leurs Plénipotentiaires, savoir:

(*As to the names, see the Acte Final, supra, p.* 84.)

Lesquels, après avoir déposé leurs pleins pouvoirs, trouvés en bonne et due forme, sont convenus des dispositions suivantes:

Art. 1. Les Puissances contractantes reconnaissent que les hostilités entre elles ne doivent pas commencer sans un avertissement préalable et non équivoque, qui aura, soit la forme d'une déclaration de guerre motivée, soit celle d'un ultimatum avec déclaration de guerre conditionnelle.

Art. 2. L'état de guerre devra être notifié sans retard aux Puissances neutres et ne produira effet à leur égard qu'après réception d'une notification qui pourra être faite même par voie télégraphique. Toutefois les Puissances neutres ne pourraient invoquer l'absence de notification, s'il était établi d'une manière non douteuse qu'en fait elles connaissaient l'état de guerre.

Art. 3. L'Article 1 de la présente Convention produira effet en cas de guerre entre deux ou plusieurs des Puissances contractantes. L'Article 2 est obligatoire dans les rapports entre un belligérant contractant et les Puissances neutres également contractantes.

Art. 4. La présente Convention sera ratifiée aussitôt que possible.

Les ratifications seront déposées à La Haye.

Le premier dépôt de ratifications sera constaté par un procès-verbal signé par les représentants des Puissances qui y prennent part et par le Ministre des Affaires Étrangères des Pays-Bas.

Les dépôts ultérieurs de ratifications se feront au moyen d'une notification écrite adressée au Gouvernement des Pays-Bas et accompagnée de l'instrument de ratification.

Copie certifiée conforme du procès-verbal relatif au premier dépôt de ratifications, des notifications mentionnées à l'alinéa précédent ainsi que des instruments de ratification, sera immédiatement remise par les soins du Gouvernement des Pays-Bas et par la voie diplomatique aux Puissances conviées à la Deuxième Conférence de la Paix, ainsi qu'aux autres Puissances qui auront adhéré à la Convention. Dans les cas visés par l'alinéa précédent, ledit Gouvernement leur fera connaître en même temps la date à laquelle il a reçu la notification.

Art. 5. Les Puissances non signataires sont admises à adhérer à la présente Convention.

La Puissance qui désire adhérer notifie par écrit son intention au Gouvernement des Pays-Bas en lui transmettant l'acte d'adhésion qui sera déposé dans les archives dudit Gouvernement.

Ce Gouvernement transmettra immédiatement à toutes les autres Puissances copie certifiée conforme de la notification ainsi que de l'acte d'adhésion, en indiquant la date à laquelle il a reçu la notification.

Art. 6. La présente Convention produira effet, pour les Puissances qui auront participé au premier dépôt de ratifications, soixante jours après la date du procès-verbal de ce dépôt, et, pour les Puissances qui ratifieront ultérieurement ou qui adhéreront, soixante jours après que la notification de leur ratification ou de leur adhésion aura été reçue par le Gouvernement des Pays-Bas.

Art. 7. S'il arrivait qu'une des Hautes Parties Contractantes voulût dénoncer la présente Convention, la dénonciation sera notifiée par écrit au Gouvernement des Pays-Bas qui communiquera immédiatement copie certifiée conforme de la notification à toutes les autres Puissances en leur faisant savoir la date à laquelle il l'a reçue.

La dénonciation ne produira ses effets qu'à l'égard de la Puissance qui l'aura notifiée et un an après que la notification en sera parvenue au Gouvernement des Pays-Bas.

Art. 8. Un registre tenu par le Ministère des Affaires Étrangères des Pays-Bas indiquera la date du dépôt de ratifications effectué en vertu de l'Article 4, alinéas 3 et 4, ainsi que la date à laquelle auront été reçues les notifications d'adhésion (Article 5, alinéa 2) ou de dénonciation (Article 7, alinéa 1).

Chaque Puissance contractante est admise à prendre connaissance de ce registre et à en demander des extraits certifiés conformes.

En foi de quoi, les Plénipotentiaires ont revêtu la présente Convention de leurs signatures.

Fait à La Haye, le dix-huit octobre mil neuf cent sept, en un seul exemplaire qui restera déposé dans les archives du Gouvernement des Pays-Bas et dont des copies, certifiées conformes, seront remises par la voie diplomatique aux Puissances qui ont été conviées à la Deuxième Conférence de la Paix.

TRANSLATION.

The Hague Convention No. iii of 1907, relative to the Commencement of Hostilities.

His Majesty the King of the United Kingdom of Great Britain and Ireland, and of the British Dominions beyond the Seas, Emperor of India, &c., &c., &c.

(*The list of Powers is the same as in the Acte Final, supra, p.* 84.)

Considering that it is important for the security of peaceful relations, that hostilities should not commence without previous warning;

That it is also important that a state of war should be notified without delay to neutral Powers;

Being desirous of concluding a Convention to this effect, have appointed the following as their Plenipotentiaries:

(*As to the names, see the Acte Final, supra, p.* 84.)

Who, after depositing their full powers, found in good and due form, have agreed upon the following provisions:—

(*For the regulative articles, viz.* 1 *and* 2, *see Articles* 16 *and* 17 *in the body of this work, supra, p.* 18.)

Art. 3. Article 1 of the present Convention shall take effect in case of war between two or more of the Contracting Powers. Article 2 is binding as between a belligerent Power which is a party to the Convention and neutral Powers which are also parties to the Convention.

Art. 4. The present Convention shall be ratified as soon as possible.

The ratifications shall be deposited at The Hague.

The first deposit of ratifications shall be attested by a *procès-verbal* signed by the Representatives of the Powers which take part therein and by the Minister for Foreign Affairs of the Netherlands.

The subsequent deposits of ratifications shall be made by means of a written notification addressed to the Government of the Netherlands and accompanied by the instrument of ratification.

A copy certified as correct of the *procès-verbal* relative to the first deposit of ratifications, of the notifications mentioned in the preceding paragraph, as well as of the instruments of ratification, shall be immediately sent by the Government of the Netherlands, and through the diplomatic channel, to the Powers invited to the Second Peace Conference, as well as to the other Powers which shall have adhered to the Convention. In the cases contemplated in the preceding paragraph, the said Government shall at the same time inform them of the date on which it has received the notification.

Art. 5. Non-Signatory Powers are admitted to adhere to the present Convention.

The Power which desires to adhere notifies in writing its intention to the Government of the Netherlands, forwarding to it the act of adhesion, which shall be deposited in the archives of the said Government.

This Government shall at once forward to all the other Powers a copy certified as correct of the notification as well as of the act of adhesion, mentioning the date on which it received the notification.

Art. 6. The present Convention shall come into force, for the Powers which shall have taken part in the first deposit of ratifications, sixty days after the date of the *procès-verbal* of that deposit, and, in the case of the Powers which ratify subsequently or which adhere, sixty days after the notification of their ratification or of their adhesion shall have been received by the Government of the Netherlands.

Art. 7. In the event of one of the High Contracting Parties wishing to denounce the present Convention, the denunciation shall be notified in writing to the Government of the Netherlands, which shall immediately communicate a copy certified as correct of the notification to all the other Powers, informing them of the date on which it was received.

The denunciation shall take effect only with reference to the notifying Power, and one year after the notification shall have reached the Government of the Netherlands.

Art. 8. A register kept by the Ministry for Foreign Affairs of the Netherlands shall give the date of the deposit of ratifications made in virtue of Article 5, paragraphs 3 and 4, as well as the date on which the notifications of adhesion (Article 6, paragraph 2) or of denunciation (Article 8, paragraph 1) shall have been received.

Each Contracting Power is entitled to inspect this register and to be supplied with extracts from it certified as correct.

In faith whereof the Plenipotentiaries have appended their signatures to the present Convention.

Done at The Hague, the 18th October, 1907, in a single copy, which shall remain deposited in the archives of the Government of the Netherlands, and copies of which certified as correct shall be sent, through the diplomatic channel, to the Powers which have been invited to the Second Peace Conference.

CONVENTION No. iv.

CONCERNANT LES LOIS ET COUTUMES DE LA GUERRE SUR TERRE.

Sa Majesté le Roi du Royaume-Uni de Grande-Bretagne et d'Irlande, et des Territoires Britanniques au delà des mers, Empereur des Indes, &c., &c., &c.

(*The list of Powers is the same as in the Acte Final, supra, p.* 84.)

Considérant que, tout en recherchant les moyens de sauvegarder la paix et de prévenir les conflits armés entre les nations, il importe de se préoccuper également du cas où l'appel aux armes serait amené par des événements que leur sollicitude n'aurait pu détourner;

Animés du désir de servir encore, dans cette hypothèse extrême, les intérêts de l'humanité et les exigences toujours progressives de la civilisation;

Estimant qu'il importe, à cette fin, de réviser les lois et coutumes générales de la guerre, soit dans le but de les définir avec plus de précision, soit afin d'y tracer certaines limites destinées à en restreindre autant que possible les rigueurs;

Ont jugé nécessaire de compléter et de préciser sur certains points l'œuvre de la Première Conférence de la Paix qui, s'inspirant, à la suite de la Conférence de Bruxelles de 1874, de ces idées recommandées par une sage et généreuse prévoyance, a adopté des dispositions ayant pour objet de définir et de régler les usages de la guerre sur terre.

Selon les vues des Hautes Parties Contractantes, ces dispositions, dont la rédaction a été inspirée par le désir de diminuer les maux de la guerre, autant que les nécessités militaires le permettent, sont destinées à servir de règle générale de conduite aux belligérants, dans leurs rapports entre eux et avec les populations.

Il n'a pas été possible toutefois de concerter dès maintenant des stipulations s'étendant à toutes les circonstances qui se présentent dans la pratique;

D'autre part, il ne pouvait entrer dans les intentions des Hautes Parties Contractantes que les cas non prévus fussent, faute de stipulation écrite, laissés à l'appréciation arbitraire de ceux qui dirigent les armées.

En attendant qu'un Code plus complet des lois de la guerre puisse être édicté, les Hautes Parties Contractantes jugent opportun de constater que, dans les cas non compris dans les dispositions réglementaires adoptées par Elles, les populations et les belligérants restent sous la sauvegarde et sous l'empire des principes du droit des gens, tels qu'ils résultent des usages établis entre nations civilisées, des lois de l'humanité et des exigences de la conscience publique.

Elles déclarent que c'est dans ce sens que doivent s'entendre notamment les Articles 1 et 2 du Règlement adopté.

Les Hautes Parties Contractantes, désirant conclure une nouvelle Convention à cet effet, ont nommé pour Leurs Plénipotentiaires, savoir:

(*As to the names, see the Acte Final, supra, p.* 84.)

Lesquels, après avoir déposé leurs pleins pouvoirs, trouvés en bonne et due forme, sont convenus de ce qui suit:

Art. 1. Les Puissances contractantes donneront à leurs forces armées de terre des instructions qui seront conformes au Règlement concernant les lois et coutumes de la guerre sur terre, annexé à la présente Convention.

Art. 2. Les dispositions contenues dans le Règlement visé à l'Article 1er, ainsi que dans la présente Convention, ne sont applicables qu'entre les Puissances contractantes et seulement si les belligérants sont tous parties à la Convention.

Art. 3. La Partie belligérante qui violerait les dispositions dudit Règlement sera tenue à indemnité, s'il y a lieu, Elle sera responsable de tous actes commis par les personnes faisant partie de sa force armée.

Art. 4. La présente Convention dûment ratifiée remplacera, dans les rapports entre les Puissances contractantes, la Convention du 29 juillet 1899 concernant les lois et coutumes de la guerre sur terre.

La Convention de 1899 reste en vigueur dans les rapports entre les Puissances qui l'ont signée et qui ne ratifieraient pas également la présente Convention.

Art. 5. La présente Convention sera ratifiée aussitôt que possible.

Les ratifications seront déposées à La Haye.

Le premier dépôt de ratifications sera constaté par un procès-verbal signé par les représentants des Puissances qui y prennent part et par le Ministre des Affaires Étrangères des Pays-Bas.

Les dépôts ultérieurs de ratifications se feront au moyen d'une notification écrite adressée au Gouvernement des Pays-Bas et accompagnée de l'instrument de ratification.

Copie certifiée conforme du procès-verbal relatif au premier dépôt de ratifications, des notifications mentionnées à l'alinéa précédent, ainsi que des instruments de ratification, sera immédiatement remise par les soins du Gouvernement des Pays-Bas et par la voie diplomatique aux Puissances conviées à la Deuxième Conférence de la Paix, ainsi qu'aux autres Puissances qui auront adhéré à la Convention. Dans les cas visés par l'alinéa précédent, ledit Gouvernement leur fera connaître en même temps la date à laquelle il a reçu la notification.

Art. 6. Les Puissances non signataires sont admises à adhérer à la présente Convention.

La Puissance qui désire adhérer notifie par écrit son intention au Gouvernement des Pays-Bas en lui transmettant l'acte d'adhésion qui sera déposé dans les archives dudit Gouvernement.

Ce Gouvernement transmettra immédiatement à toutes les autres Puissances copie certifiée conforme de la notification ainsi que de l'acte d'adhésion, en indiquant la date à laquelle il a reçu la notification.

Art. 7. La présente Convention produira effet, pour les Puissances qui auront participé au premier dépôt de ratifications, soixante jours après la date du procès-verbal de ce dépôt, et, pour les Puissances qui ratifieront ultérieurement ou qui adhéreront, soixante jours après que la notification de leur ratification ou de leur adhésion aura été reçue par le Gouvernement des Pays-Bas.

Art. 8. S'il arrivait qu'une des Puissances contractantes voulût dénoncer la présente Convention, la dénonciation sera notifiée par écrit au Gouvernement des Pays-Bas, qui communiquera immédiatement copie certifiée conforme de la notification à toutes les autres Puissances en leur faisant savoir la date à laquelle il l'a reçue.

La dénonciation ne produira ses effets qu'à l'égard de la Puissance qui l'aura notifiée et un an après que la notification en sera parvenue au Gouvernement des Pays-Bas.

Art. 9. Un registre tenu par le Ministère des Affaires Étrangères des Pays-Bas indiquera la date du dépôt de ratifications effectué en vertu de l'Article 5, alinéas 3 et 4, ainsi que la date à laquelle auront été reçues les notifications d'adhésion (Article 6, alinéa 2), ou de dénonciation (Article 8, alinéa 1).

Chaque Puissance contractante est admise à prendre connaissance de ce registre et à en demander des extraits certifiés conformes.

En foi de quoi, les Plénipotentiaires ont revêtu la présente Convention de leurs signatures.

Fait à La Haye, le dix-huit octobre mil neuf cent sept, en un seul exemplaire qui restera déposé dans les archives du Gouvernement des Pays-Bas et dont des copies, certifiées conformes, seront remises par la voie diplomatique aux Puissances qui ont été conviées à la Deuxième Conférence de la Paix.

ANNEXE À LA CONVENTION.

RÈGLEMENT CONCERNANT LES LOIS ET COUTUMES DE LA GUERRE SUR TERRE.

SECTION PREMIÈRE. DES BELLIGÉRANTS.

CHAPITRE PREMIER. *De la qualité de belligérant.*

Art. 1. Les lois, les droits et les devoirs de la guerre ne s'appliquent pas seulement à l'armée, mais encore aux milices et aux corps de volontaires réunissant les conditions suivantes :

1° d'avoir à leur tête une personne responsable pour ses subordonnés ;

2° d'avoir un signe distinctif fixe et reconnaissable à distance ;

3° de porter les armes ouvertement et

4° de se conformer dans leurs opérations aux lois et coutumes de la guerre.

Dans les pays où les milices ou des corps de volontaires constituent l'armée ou en font partie, ils sont compris sous la dénomination d'*armée.*

Art. 2. La population d'un territoire non occupé qui, à l'approche de l'ennemi, prend spontanément les armes pour combattre les troupes d'invasion sans avoir eu le temps de s'organiser conformément à l'Article premier, sera considérée comme belligérante si elle porte les armes ouvertement et si elle respecte les lois et coutumes de la guerre.

Art. 3. Les forces armées des Parties belligérantes peuvent se composer de combattants et de non-combattants. En cas de capture par l'ennemi, les uns et les autres ont droit au traitement des prisonniers de guerre.

CHAPITRE II. *Des prisonniers de guerre.*

Art. 4. Les prisonniers de guerre sont au pouvoir du Gouvernement ennemi, mais non des individus ou des corps qui les ont capturés.

Ils doivent être traités avec humanité.

Tout ce qui leur appartient personnellement, excepté les armes, les chevaux et les papiers militaires, reste leur propriété.

Art. 5. Les prisonniers de guerre peuvent être assujettis à

l'internement dans une ville, forteresse, camp ou localité quelconque, avec obligation de ne pas s'en éloigner au delà de certaines limites déterminées ; mais ils ne peuvent être enfermés que par mesure de sûreté indispensable, et seulement pendant la durée des circonstances qui nécessitent cette mesure.

Art. 6. L'État peut employer, comme travailleurs, les prisonniers de guerre, selon leur grade et leurs aptitudes, à l'exception des officiers. Ces travaux ne seront pas excessifs et n'auront aucun rapport avec les opérations de la guerre.

Les prisonniers peuvent être autorisés à travailler pour le compte d'administrations publiques ou de particuliers, ou pour leur propre compte.

Les travaux faits pour l'État sont payés d'après les tarifs en vigueur pour les militaires de l'armée nationale exécutant les mêmes travaux, ou, s'il n'en existe pas, d'après un tarif en rapport avec les travaux exécutés.

Lorsque les travaux ont lieu pour le compte d'autres administrations publiques ou pour des particuliers, les conditions en sont réglées d'accord avec l'autorité militaire.

Le salaire des prisonniers contribuera à adoucir leur position, et le surplus leur sera compté au moment de leur libération, sauf défalcation des frais d'entretien.

Art. 7. Le Gouvernement au pouvoir duquel se trouvent les prisonniers de guerre est chargé de leur entretien.

A défaut d'une entente spéciale entre les belligérants, les prisonniers de guerre seront traités pour la nourriture, le couchage et l'habillement, sur le même pied que les troupes du Gouvernement qui les aura capturés.

Art. 8. Les prisonniers de guerre seront soumis aux lois, règlements et ordres en vigueur dans l'armée de l'État au pouvoir duquel ils se trouvent. Tout acte d'insubordination autorise, à leur égard, les mesures de rigueur nécessaires.

Les prisonniers évadés, qui seraient repris avant d'avoir pu rejoindre leur armée ou avant de quitter le territoire occupé par l'armée qui les aura capturés, sont passibles de peines disciplinaires.

Les prisonniers qui, après avoir réussi à s'évader, sont de nouveau faits prisonniers, ne sont passibles d'aucune peine pour la fuite antérieure.

Art. 9. Chaque prisonnier de guerre est tenu de déclarer, s'il est interrogé à ce sujet, ses véritables noms et grade et, dans le cas où il enfreindrait cette règle, il s'exposerait à une restriction des avantages accordés aux prisonniers de guerre de sa catégorie.

Art. 10. Les prisonniers de guerre peuvent être mis en liberté sur parole, si les lois de leur pays les y autorisent, et, en pareil cas, ils sont obligés, sous la garantie de leur honneur personnel, de remplir scrupuleusement, tant vis-à-vis de leur propre Gouvernement que vis-à-vis de celui qui les a faits prisonniers, les engagements qu'ils auraient contractés.

Dans le même cas, leur propre Gouvernement est tenu de n'exiger ni accepter d'eux aucun service contraire à la parole donnée.

Art. 11. Un prisonnier de guerre ne peut être contraint d'accepter sa liberté sur parole; de même le Gouvernement ennemi n'est pas obligé d'accéder à la demande du prisonnier réclamant sa mise en liberté sur parole.

Art. 12. Tout prisonnier de guerre, libéré sur parole et repris portant les armes contre le Gouvernement envers lequel il s'était engagé d'honneur, ou contre les alliés de celui-ci, perd le droit au traitement des prisonniers de guerre et peut être traduit devant les tribunaux.

Art. 13. Les individus qui suivent une armée sans en faire directement partie, tels que les correspondants et les reporters de journaux, les vivandiers, les fournisseurs, qui tombent au pouvoir de l'ennemi et que celui-ci juge utile de détenir, ont droit au traitement des prisonniers de guerre, à condition qu'ils soient munis d'une légitimation de l'autorité militaire de l'armée qu'ils accompagnaient.

Art. 14. Il est constitué, dès le début des hostilités, dans chacun des États belligérants, et, le cas échéant, dans les Pays neutres qui auront recueilli des belligérants sur leur territoire, un bureau de renseignements sur les prisonniers de guerre. Ce bureau, chargé de répondre à toutes les demandes qui les concernent, reçoit des divers services compétents toutes les indications relatives aux internements et aux mutations, aux mises en liberté sur parole, aux échanges, aux évasions, aux entrées dans les hôpitaux, aux décès, ainsi que les autres renseignements nécessaires pour établir et tenir à jour une fiche individuelle pour chaque prisonnier de guerre. Le bureau devra porter sur cette fiche le numéro matricule, les nom et prénom, l'âge, le lieu d'origine, le grade, le corps de troupe, les blessures, la date et le lieu de la capture, de l'internement, des blessures et de la mort, ainsi que toutes les observations particulières. La fiche individuelle sera remise au Gouvernement de l'autre belligérant après la conclusion de la paix.

Le bureau de renseignements est également chargé de recueillir et de centraliser tous les objets d'un usage personnel, valeurs, lettres, etc., qui seront trouvés sur les champs de bataille ou délaissés par des prisonniers libérés sur parole, échangés, évadés ou décédés dans les hôpitaux et ambulances, et de les transmettre aux intéressés.

Art. 15. Les sociétés de secours pour les prisonniers de guerre, régulièrement constituées selon la loi de leur pays et ayant pour objet d'être les intermédiaires de l'action charitable, recevront, de la part des belligérants, pour elles et pour leurs agents dûment accrédités, toute facilité, dans les limites tracées par les nécessités militaires et les règles administratives, pour accomplir efficacement leur tâche d'humanité. Les délégués de ces sociétés pourront être admis à distribuer des secours dans les dépôts d'internement, ainsi qu'aux lieux d'étape des prisonniers rapatriés, moyennant une permission personnelle délivrée par l'autorité militaire, et en prenant l'engagement par écrit de se soumettre à toutes les mesures d'ordre et de police que celle-ci prescrirait.

Art. 16. Les bureaux de renseignements jouissent de la franchise de port. Les lettres, mandats et articles d'argent, ainsi que les colis postaux destinés aux prisonniers de guerre ou expédiés par eux, seront affranchis de toutes les taxes postales, aussi bien dans les pays d'origine et de destination que dans les pays intermédiaires.

Les dons et secours en nature destinés aux prisonniers de guerre seront admis en franchise de tous droits d'entrée et autres, ainsi que des taxes de transport sur les chemins de fer exploités par l'État.

Art. 17. Les officiers prisonniers recevront la solde à laquelle ont droit les officiers de même grade du pays où ils sont retenus, à charge de remboursement par leur Gouvernement.

Art. 18. Toute latitude est laissée aux prisonniers de guerre pour l'exercice de leur religion, y compris l'assistance aux offices de leur culte, à la seule condition de se conformer aux mesures d'ordre et de police prescrites par l'autorité militaire.

Art. 19. Les testaments des prisonniers de guerre sont reçus ou dressés dans les mêmes conditions que pour les militaires de l'armée nationale.

On suivra également les mêmes règles en ce qui concerne les pièces relatives à la constatation des décès, ainsi que pour l'inhumation des prisonniers de guerre, en tenant compte de leur grade et de leur rang.

Art. 20. Après la conclusion de la paix, le rapatriement des prisonniers de guerre s'effectuera dans le plus bref délai possible.

Chapitre III. *Des malades et des blessés.*

Art. 21. Les obligations des belligérants concernant le service des malades et des blessés sont régies par la Convention de Genève.

Section II. Des Hostilités.

Chapitre premier. *Des moyens de nuire à l'ennemi, des sièges et des bombardements.*

Art. 22. Les belligérants n'ont pas un droit illimité quant au choix des moyens de nuire à l'ennemi.

Art. 23. Outre les prohibitions établies par des Conventions spéciales, il est notamment interdit:

(*a*) d'employer du poison ou des armes empoisonnées;

(*b*) de tuer ou de blesser par trahison des individus appartenant à la nation ou à l'armée ennemie;

(*c*) de tuer ou de blesser un ennemi qui, ayant mis bas les armes ou n'ayant plus les moyens de se défendre, s'est rendu à discrétion;

(*d*) de déclarer qu'il ne sera pas fait de quartier;

(*e*) d'employer des armes, des projectiles ou des matières propres à causer des maux superflus;

(*f*) d'user indûment du pavillon parlementaire, du pavillon national ou des insignes militaires et de l'uniforme de l'ennemi, ainsi que des signes distinctifs de la Convention de Genève;

(*g*) de détruire ou de saisir des propriétés ennemies, sauf les cas où ces destructions ou ces saisies seraient impérieusement commandées par les nécessités de la guerre;

(*h*) de déclarer éteints, suspendus ou non recevables en justice, les droits et actions des nationaux de la Partie adverse.

Il est également interdit à un belligérant de forcer les nationaux de la Partie adverse à prendre part aux opérations de guerre dirigées contre leur pays, même dans le cas où ils auraient été à son service avant le commencement de la guerre.

Art. 24. Les ruses de guerre et l'emploi des moyens nécessaires pour se procurer des renseignements sur l'ennemi et sur le terrain sont considérés comme licites.

Art. 25. Il est interdit d'attaquer ou de bombarder, par quelque moyen que ce soit, des villes, villages, habitations ou bâtiments qui ne sont pas défendus.

Art. 26. Le commandant des troupes assaillantes, avant d'entreprendre le bombardement, et sauf le cas d'attaque de vive force, devra faire tout ce qui dépend de lui pour en avertir les autorités.

Art. 27. Dans les sièges et bombardements, toutes les mesures nécessaires doivent être prises pour épargner, autant que possible, les édifices cousacrés aux cultes, aux arts, aux sciences et à la bienfaisance, les monuments historiques, les hôpitaux et les lieux de rassemblement de malades et de blessés, à condition qu'ils ne soient pas employés en même temps à un but militaire.

Le devoir des assiégés est de désigner ces édifices ou lieux de rassemblement par des signes visibles spéciaux qui seront notifiés d'avance à l'assiégeant.

Art. 28. Il est interdit de livrer au pillage une ville ou localité même prise d'assaut.

Chapitre II. *Des espions.*

Art. 29. Ne peut être considéré comme espion que l'individu qui, agissant clandestinement ou sous de faux prétextes, recueille ou cherche à recueillir des informations dans la zone d'opérations d'un belligérant, avec l'intention de les communiquer à la Partie adverse.

Ainsi les militaires non déguisés qui ont pénétré dans la zone d'opérations de l'armée ennemie, à l'effet de recueillir des informations, ne sont pas considérés comme espions. De même, ne sont pas considérés comme espions: les militaires et les non militaires, accomplissant ouvertement leur mission, chargés de transmettre des dépêches destinées, soit à leur propre armée, soit à l'armée ennemie. A cette catégorie appartiennent également les individus envoyés en ballon pour transmettre les dépêches, et, en général, pour entretenir les communications entre les diverses parties d'une armée ou d'un territoire.

Art. 30. L'espion pris sur le fait ne pourra être puni sans jugement préalable.

Art. 31. L'espion qui, ayant rejoint l'armée à laquelle il appartient, est capturé plus tard par l'ennemi, est traité comme prisonnier de guerre et n'encourt aucune responsabilité pour ses actes d'espionnage antérieurs.

Chapitre III. *Des parlementaires.*

Art. 32. Est considéré comme parlementaire l'individu autorisé par l'un des belligérants à entrer en pourparlers avec l'autre et se présentant avec le drapeau blanc. Il a droit à l'inviolabilité ainsi que le trompette, clairon ou tambour, le porte-drapeau et l'interprète qui l'accompagneraient.

Art. 33. Le chef auquel un parlementaire est expédié n'est pas obligé de le recevoir en toutes circonstances.

Il peut prendre toutes les mesures nécessaires afin d'empêcher le parlementaire de profiter de sa mission pour se renseigner.

Il a le droit, en cas d'abus, de retenir temporairement le parlementaire.

Art. 34. Le parlementaire perd ses droits d'inviolabilité, s'il est prouvé, d'une manière positive et irrécusable, qu'il a profité de sa position privilégiée pour provoquer ou commettre un acte de trahison.

Chapitre IV. *Des capitulations.*

Art. 35. Les capitulations arrêtées entre les Parties contractantes doivent tenir compte des règles de l'honneur militaire.

Une fois fixées, elles doivent être scrupuleusement observées par les deux Parties.

Chapitre V. *De l'armistice.*

Art. 36. L'armistice suspend les opérations de guerre par un accord mutuel des Parties belligérantes. Si la durée n'en est pas déterminée, les Parties belligérantes peuvent reprendre en tout temps les opérations, pourvu toutefois que l'ennemi soit averti en temps convenu, conformément aux conditions de l'armistice.

Art. 37. L'armistice peut être général ou local. Le premier suspend partout les opérations de guerre des États belligérants; le second, seulement entre certaines fractions des armées belligérantes et dans un rayon déterminé.

Art. 38. L'armistice doit être notifié officiellement et en temps utile aux Autorités compétentes et aux troupes. Les hostilités sont suspendues immédiatement après la notification ou au terme fixé.

Art. 39. Il dépend des Parties contractantes de fixer, dans les clauses de l'armistice, les rapports qui pourraient avoir lieu, sur le théâtre de la guerre, avec les populations et entre elles.

Art. 40. Toute violation grave de l'armistice, par l'une des Parties, donne à l'autre le droit de le dénoncer et même, en cas d'urgence, de reprendre immédiatement les hostilités.

Art. 41. La violation des clauses de l'armistice, par des particuliers agissant de leur propre initiative, donne droit seulement à réclamer la punition des coupables et, s'il y a lieu, une indemnité pour les pertes éprouvées.

SECTION III. DE L'AUTORITÉ MILITAIRE SUR LE TERRITOIRE DE L'ÉTAT ENNEMI.

Art. 42. Un territoire est considéré comme occupé lorsqu'il se trouve placé de fait sous l'autorité de l'armée ennemie.

L'occupation ne s'étend qu'aux territoires où cette autorité est établie et en mesure de s'exercer.

Art. 43. L'autorité du pouvoir légal ayant passé de fait entre les mains de l'occupant, celui-ci prendra toutes les mesures qui dépendent de lui en vue de rétablir et d'assurer, autant qu'il est possible, l'ordre et la vie publics en respectant, sauf empêchement absolu, les lois en vigueur dans le pays.

Art. 44. Il est interdit à un belligérant de forcer la population d'un territoire occupé à donner des renseignements sur l'armée de l'autre belligérant ou sur ses moyens de défense.

Art. 45. Il est interdit de contraindre la population d'un territoire occupé à prêter serment à la Puissance ennemie.

Art. 46. L'honneur et les droits de la famille, la vie des individus et la propriété privée, ainsi que les convictions religieuses et l'exercice des cultes, doivent être respectés.

La propriété privée ne peut pas être confisquée.

Art. 47. Le pillage est formellement interdit.

Art. 48. Si l'occupant prélève, dans le territoire occupé, les impôts, droits et péages établis au profit de l'État, il le fera, autant que possible, d'après les règles de l'assiette et de la répartition en vigueur, et il en résultera pour lui l'obligation de pourvoir aux frais de l'administration du territoire occupé dans la mesure où le Gouvernement légal y était tenu.

Art. 49. Si, en dehors des impôts visés à l'Article précédent, l'occupant prélève d'autres contributions en argent dans le territoire occupé, ce ne pourra être que pour les besoins de l'armée ou de l'administration de ce territoire.

Art. 50. Aucune peine collective, pécuniaire ou autre, ne pourra être édictée contre les populations à raison de faits individuels dont elles ne pourraient être considérées comme solidairement responsables.

Art. 51. Aucune contribution ne sera perçue qu'en vertu d'un ordre écrit et sous la responsabilité d'un général en chef.

Il ne sera procédé, autant que possible, à cette perception que d'après les règles de l'assiette et de la répartition des impôts en vigueur.

Pour toute contribution, un reçu sera délivré aux contribuables.

Art. 52. Des réquisitions en nature et des services ne pourront être réclamés des communes ou des habitants que pour les besoins de l'armée d'occupation. Ils seront en rapport avec les ressources du pays et de telle nature qu'ils n'impliquent pas pour les populations l'obligation de prendre part aux opérations de la guerre contre leur patrie.

Ces réquisitions et ces services ne seront réclamés qu'avec l'autorisation du commandant dans la localité occupée.

Les prestations en nature seront, autant que possible, payées au comptant; sinon, elles seront constatées par des reçus, et le paiement des sommes dues sera effectué le plus tôt possible.

Art. 53. L'armée qui occupe un territoire ne pourra saisir que le numéraire, les fonds et les valeurs exigibles appartenant en propre à l'État, les dépôts d'armes, moyens de transport, magasins et approvisionnements et, en général, toute propriété mobilière de l'État de nature à servir aux opérations de la guerre.

Tous les moyens affectés sur terre, sur mer et dans les airs à la transmission des nouvelles, au transport des personnes ou des choses, en dehors des cas régis par le droit maritime, les dépôts d'armes et, en général, toute espèce de munitions de guerre, peuvent être saisis, même s'ils appartiennent à des personnes privées, mais devront être restitués et les indemnités seront réglées à la paix.

Art. 54. Les câbles sous-marins reliant un territoire occupé à un territoire neutre ne seront saisis ou détruits que dans le cas d'une nécessité absolue. Ils devront également être restitués et les indemnités seront réglées à la paix.

Art. 55. L'État occupant ne se considérera que comme administrateur et usufruitier des édifices publics, immeubles, forêts et exploitations agricoles appartenant à l'État ennemi et se trouvant dans le pays occupé. Il devra sauvegarder le fonds de ces propriétés et les administrer conformément aux règles de l'usufruit.

Art. 56. Les biens des communes, ceux des établissements consacrés aux cultes, à la charité et à l'instruction, aux arts et aux sciences, même appartenant à l'État, seront traités comme la propriété privée.

Toute saisie, destruction ou dégradation intentionnelle de semblables établissements, de monuments historiques, d'œuvres d'art et de science, est interdite et doit être poursuivie.

TRANSLATION.

The Hague Convention No. iv of 1907, respecting the Laws and Customs of War on Land.

H.M. the King of Great Britain and Ireland, &c., &c., &c.

(*The list of Powers is the same as in the Acte Final, supra, p.* 84.)

Considering that, while seeking means to preserve peace and prevent armed conflicts among nations, it is a duty to have regard likewise to the case where an appeal to arms may be brought about by events which their care shall not have been able to avert;

Animated by the desire to serve, even in this extreme supposition, the interests of humanity and the ever increasing requirements of civilization;

Thinking it to be a duty, with this object, to revise the general laws and customs of war, both with a view to define them more precisely, and in order to place certain limits upon them for the purpose of modifying their severity as far as possible;

Have thought it necessary to complete and make more definite on certain points the work of the First Peace Conference, which inspired, after the Brussels Conference of 1874, by these views, commended by a wise and generous foresight, adopted provisions, the object of which was to define and regulate the usages of war on land.

In the view of the High Contracting Parties, these provisions, the wording of which was inspired by a desire to diminish the evils of war, so far as military necessities permit, are intended to serve as general rules of conduct for belligerents in their relations with each other and with populations.

It has not, however, been possible to agree forthwith on provisions covering all the circumstances which occur in practice.

On the other hand, it could not be intended by the High Contracting Parties that the cases not provided for should, for want of a written provision, be left to the arbitrary judgement of military commanders.

Until a more complete code of the laws of war can be authorized, the High Contracting Parties think it desirable to declare that in cases not included in the Regulations adopted by them, populations and belligerents remain under the protection and government of the principles of international law, deducible from the usages established between civilized nations, from the laws of humanity, and from the requirements of the public conscience.

They declare that it is in this sense that Articles 1 and 2 especially of the Regulations adopted must be understood.

The High Contracting Parties, desiring to conclude a Convention to this effect, have appointed as their Plenipotentiaries, to wit:—

(*As to the names of the Plenipotentiaries, see the Acte Final, supra, p.* 84.)

Who, after deposit of their full powers, found to be in good and due form, have agreed as follows:—

Art. 1. The Contracting Powers will issue instructions to their armed land forces, which shall be in conformity with the 'Regulations respecting the Laws and Customs of War on Land' annexed to the present Convention.

Art. 2. The provisions of the Regulations mentioned in Article 1, as also those of this Convention, are binding only on the Contracting Powers, and only when all the belligerents are parties to the Convention.

(*Art.* 3 *is Art.* 19 *of the present work, see supra, p.* 19.)

Art. 4. The present Convention, when duly ratified, shall replace, in the mutual relations of the Contracting Powers, the Convention of July 29, 1899, concerning the laws and customs of war on land.

The Convention of 1899 remains in force between the Powers which have signed it, and shall not also ratify the present Convention.

(*Arts.* 5 *to* 8 *are identical with Arts.* 4 *to* 7 *of* H iii, *supra, pp.* 92, 93.)

Art. 9. A Register, kept by the Minister for Foreign Affairs of the Netherlands, shall mention the date of the deposit of ratifications made in pursuance of Art. 5, paragraphs 3 and 4, as also the date at which notifications of adhesion (Art. 6, par. 2), or of denunciation (Art. 8, par. 1), shall have been received. Each Contracting Power is at liberty to have access to this Register and to ask for extracts from it certified as correct.

In faith of which the Plenipotentiaries have signed the present Convention and affixed their seals thereto.

Done at The Hague, the 18th October, 1907, in a single copy, which shall be kept in the archives of the Government of the Netherlands, and copies of which, certified as correct, shall be forwarded through the diplomatic channels, to the Powers which have been invited to the Second Peace Conference.

ANNEX TO THE CONVENTION.

(*Containing the Regulations*, 1–56, *which are printed as Articles* 21–41, 70, 76–84, 86, 87, 89–98, 102–116, *of the present work.*)

CONVENTION DE GENÈVE (1906)

POUR L'AMÉLIORATION DU SORT DES BLESSÉS ET MALADES DANS LES ARMÉES EN CAMPAGNE.

Sa Majesté le Roi du Royaume-Uni de la Grande-Bretagne et d'Irlande, Empereur des Indes ;

&c., &c., &c.*

Également animés du désir de diminuer, autant qu'il dépend d'eux, les maux inséparables de la guerre et voulant, dans ce but, perfectionner et compléter les dispositions convenues à Genève, le 22 août 1864, pour l'amélioration du sort des militaires blessés ou malades dans les armées en campagne,

Ont résolu de conclure une nouvelle Convention à cet effet, et ont nommé pour leurs Plénipotentiaires, savoir :

Sa Majesté le Roi du Royaume-Uni de Grande-Bretagne et d'Irlande, Empereur des Indes :

M. le major-général Sir John Charles Ardagh, K.C.M.G., K.C.I.E., C.B.

* For lists of the other Powers and names of their Plenipotentiaries, see *Parl. Paper* [Cd. 3933], 1908. For signatures, ratifications and accessions, see *infra*, Appendix IV, p. 140.

M. le Professeur Thomas Erskine Holland, K.C., D.C.L.

Sir John Furley, C.B.

M. le lieutenant-colonel William Grant Macpherson, C.M.G., R.A.M.C.

&c., &c., &c.

Lesquels, après s'être communiqué leurs pleins pouvoirs, trouvés en bonne et due forme, sont convenus de ce qui suit :

Chapitre premier. *Des blessés et malades.*

Art. 1. Les militaires et les autres personnes officiellement attachées aux armées, qui seront blessés ou malades, devront être respectés et soignés, sans distinction de nationalité, par le belligérant qui les aura en son pouvoir.

Toutefois, le belligérant, obligé d'abandonner des malades ou des blessés à son adversaire, laissera avec eux, autant que les circonstances militaires le permettront, une partie de son personnel et de son matériel sanitaires pour contribuer à les soigner.

Art. 2. Sous réserve des soins à leur fournir en vertu de l'Article précédent, les blessés ou malades d'une armée tombés au pouvoir de l'autre belligérant sont prisonniers de guerre et les règles générales du droit des gens concernant les prisonniers leur sont applicables.

Cependant, les belligérants restent libres de stipuler entre eux, à l'égard des prisonniers blessés et malades, telles clauses d'exception ou de faveur qu'ils jugeront utiles ; ils auront, notamment, la faculté de convenir :

De se remettre réciproquement, après un combat, les blessés laissés sur le champ de bataille ;

De renvoyer dans leur pays, après les avoir mis en état d'être transportés ou après guérison, les blessés ou malades qu'ils ne voudront pas garder prisonniers ;

De remettre à un État neutre, du consentement de celui-ci, des blessés ou malades de la partie adverse, à la charge par l'État neutre de les interner jusqu'à la fin des hostilités.

Art. 3. Après chaque combat, l'occupant du champ de bataille prendra des mesures pour rechercher les blessés et pour les faire protéger ainsi que les morts contre le pillage et les mauvais traitements.

Il veillera à ce que l'inhumation ou l'incinération des morts soit précédée d'un examen attentif de leurs cadavres.

Art. 4. Chaque belligérant enverra, dès qu'il sera possible, aux Autorités de leur pays ou de leur armée les marques ou pièces militaires d'identité trouvées sur les morts et l'état nominatif des blessés ou malades recueillis par lui.

Les belligérants se tiendront réciproquement au courant des internements et des mutations, ainsi que des entrées dans les hôpitaux et des décès survenus parmi les blessés et malades en leur pouvoir. Ils recueilleront tous les objets d'un usage personnel, valeurs, lettres, &c. qui seront trouvés sur les champs de bataille ou délaissés par les blessés ou malades décédés dans les établissements et formations sanitaires, pour les faire transmettre aux intéressés par les Autorités de leur pays.

Art. 5. L'Autorité militaire pourra faire appel au zèle charitable des habitants pour recueillir et soigner, sous son contrôle, des blessés ou malades des armées, en accordant aux personnes ayant répondu à cet appel une protection spéciale et certaines immunités.

Chapitre II. *Des formations et établissements sanitaires.*

Art. 6. Les formations sanitaires mobiles (c'est-à-dire celles qui sont destinées à accompagner les armées en campagne) et les établissements fixes du service de santé seront respectés et protégés par les belligérants.

Art. 7. La protection due aux formations et établissements sanitaires et à leur matériel cesse si l'on en use pour commettre des actes nuisibles à l'ennemi.

Art. 8. Ne sont pas considérés comme étant de nature à priver une formation ou un établissement sanitaire de la protection assurée par l'Article 6 :

1° Le fait que le personnel de la formation ou de l'établissement est armé et qu'il use de ses armes pour sa propre défense ou celle de ses malades et blessés ;

2° Le fait qu'à défaut d'infirmiers armés la formation est gardée par un piquet ou des sentinelles munis d'un mandat régulier ;

3° Le fait qu'il est trouvé dans la formation des armes et cartouches retirées des blessés et n'ayant pas encore été versées au service compétent.

Chapitre III. *Du personnel.*

Art. 9. Le personnel exclusivement affecté à l'enlèvement, au transport et au traitement des blessés et des malades, ainsi qu'à l'administration des formations et établissements sanitaires, les aumôniers attachés aux armées, seront respectés et protégés en toute circonstance ; s'ils tombent entre les mains de l'ennemi, ils ne seront pas traités comme prisonniers de guerre.

Ces dispositions s'appliquent au personnel de garde des formations et établissements sanitaires dans le cas prévu à l'Article 8, nº 2.

Art. 10. Est assimilé au personnel visé à l'Article précédent le personnel des Sociétés de secours volontaires dûment reconnues et autorisées par leur Gouvernement, qui sera employé dans les formations et établissements sanitaires des armées, sous la réserve que ledit personnel sera soumis aux lois et règlements militaires.

Chaque État doit notifier à l'autre, soit dès le temps de paix, soit à l'ouverture ou au cours des hostilités, en tout cas avant tout emploi effectif, les noms des Sociétés qu'il a autorisées à prêter leur concours, sous sa responsabilité, au service sanitaire officiel de ses armées.

Art. 11. Une Société reconnue d'un pays neutre ne peut prêter le concours de ses personnels et formations sanitaires à un belligérant qu'avec l'assentiment préalable de son propre Gouvernement et l'autorisation du belligérant lui-même.

Le belligérant qui a accepté le secours est tenu, avant tout emploi, d'en faire la notification à son ennemi.

Art. 12. Les personnes désignées dans les Articles 9, 10 et 11 continueront, après qu'elles seront tombées au pouvoir de l'ennemi, à remplir leurs fonctions sous sa direction.

Lorsque leur concours ne sera plus indispensable, elles seront renvoyées à leur armée ou à leur pays dans les délais et suivant l'itinéraire compatibles avec les nécessités militaires.

Elles emporteront, alors, les effets, les instruments, les armes et les chevaux qui sont leur propriété particulière.

Art. 13. L'ennemi assurera au personnel visé par l'Article 9, pendant qu'il sera en son pouvoir, les mêmes allocations et la même solde qu'au personnel des mêmes grades de son armée.

CHAPITRE IV. *Du matériel.*

Art. 14. Les formations sanitaires mobiles conserveront, si elles tombent au pouvoir de l'ennemi, leur matériel, y compris les attelages, quels que soient les moyens de transport et le personnel conducteur.

Toutefois, l'autorité militaire compétente aura la faculté de s'en servir pour les soins des blessés et malades ; la restitution du matériel aura lieu dans les conditions prévues pour le personnel sanitaire, et autant que possible en même temps.

Art. 15. Les bâtiments et le matériel des établissements fixes demeurent soumis aux lois de la guerre, mais ne pourront être détournés de leur emploi, tant qu'ils sont nécessaires aux blessés et aux malades.

Toutefois, les commandants des troupes d'opérations pourront en disposer, en cas de nécessités militaires importantes, en assurant au préalable le sort des blessés et malades qui s'y trouvent.

Art. 16. Le matériel des Sociétés de secours, admises au bénéfice de la Convention conformément aux conditions déterminées par celle-ci, est considéré comme propriété privée, et, comme tel, respecté en toute circonstance, sauf le droit de réquisition reconnu aux belligérants selon les lois et usages de la guerre.

Chapitre V. *Des convois d'évacuation.*

Art. 17. Les convois d'évacuation seront traités comme les formations sanitaires mobiles, sauf les dispositions spéciales suivantes :

1° Le belligérant interceptant un convoi pourra, si les nécessités militaires l'exigent, le disloquer en se chargeant des malades et blessés qu'il contient.

2° Dans ce cas, l'obligation de renvoyer le personnel sanitaire, prévue à l'Article 12, sera étendue à tout le personnel militaire préposé au transport ou à la garde du convoi et muni à cet effet d'un mandat régulier.

L'obligation de rendre le matériel sanitaire, prévue à l'Article 14, s'appliquera aux trains de chemins de fer et bateaux de la navigation intérieure spécialement organisés pour les évacuations, ainsi qu'au matériel d'aménagement des voitures, trains et bateaux ordinaires appartenant au service de santé.

Les voitures militaires, autres que celles du service de santé, pourront être capturées avec leurs attelages.

Le personnel civil et les divers moyens de transport provenant de la réquisition, y compris le matériel de chemin de fer et les bateaux du commerce utilisés pour les convois, seront soumis aux règles générales du droit des gens.

Chapitre VI. *Du signe distinctif.*

Art. 18. Par hommage pour la Suisse, le signe héraldique de la croix rouge sur fond blanc, par interversion des couleurs fédérales, est maintenu comme emblème et signe distinctif du service sanitaire des armées.

Art. 19. Cet emblème figure sur les drapeaux, les brassards, ainsi que sur tout le matériel se rattachant au service sanitaire, avec la permission de l'autorité militaire compétente.

Art. 20. Le personnel protégé en vertu des Articles 9, alinéa 1er, 10 et 11, porte, fixé au bras gauche, un brassard avec croix rouge sur fond blanc, délivré et timbré par l'autorité militaire compétente, accompagné d'un certificat d'identité pour les personnes rattachées au service de santé des armées et qui n'auraient pas d'uniforme militaire.

Art. 21. Le drapeau distinctif de la Convention ne peut être arboré que sur les formations et établissements sanitaires qu'elle ordonne de respecter et avec le consentement de l'autorité militaire. Il devra être accompagné du drapeau national du belligérant dont relève la formation ou l'établissement.

Toutefois les formations sanitaires tombées au pouvoir de l'ennemi n'arboreront pas d'autre drapeau que celui de la Croix-Rouge, aussi longtemps qu'elles se trouveront dans cette situation.

Art. 22. Les formations sanitaires des pays neutres, qui, dans les conditions prévues par l'Article 11, auraient été autorisées à fournir leurs services, doivent arborer, avec le drapeau de la Convention, le drapeau du belligérant dont elles relèvent.

Les dispositions du deuxième alinéa de l'Article précédent leur sont applicables.

Art. 23. L'emblème de la croix rouge sur fond blanc et les mots *Croix-Rouge* ou *Croix de Genève* ne pourront être employés, soit en temps de paix, soit en temps de guerre, que pour protéger ou désigner les formations et établissements sanitaires, le personnel et le matériel protégés par la Convention.

Chapitre VII. *De l'application et de l'exécution de la Convention.*

Art. 24. Les dispositions de la présente Convention ne sont obligatoires que pour les Puissances contractantes, entre deux ou plusieurs d'entre elles. Ces dispositions cesseront d'être obligatoires du moment où l'une des Puissances belligérantes ne serait pas signataire de la Convention.

Art. 25. Les commandants en chef des armées belligérantes auront à pourvoir aux détails d'exécution des Articles précédents, ainsi qu'aux cas non prévus, d'après les instructions de leurs Gouvernements respectifs et conformément aux principes généraux de la présente Convention.

Art. 26. Les Gouvernements signataires prendront les mesures nécessaires pour instruire leurs troupes, et spécialement le personnel protégé, des dispositions de la présente Convention, et pour les porter à la connaissance des populations.

Chapitre VIII. *De la répression des abus et des infractions.*

Art. 27. Les Gouvernements signataires, dont la législation ne serait pas dès à présent suffisante, s'engagent à prendre ou à proposer à leurs législatures les mesures nécessaires pour empêcher en tout temps l'emploi, par des particuliers ou par des sociétés autres que celles y ayant droit en vertu de la présente Convention, des insignes ou de la dénomination de *Croix-Rouge* ou *Croix de Genève*, notamment dans un but commercial, par le moyen de marques de fabrique ou de commerce.

L'interdiction de l'emploi des insignes ou de la dénomination dont il s'agit produira son effet à partir de l'époque déterminée par chaque législation et, au plus tard, cinq ans après la mise en vigueur de la présente Convention. Dès cette mise en vigueur, il ne sera plus licite de prendre une marque de fabrique ou de commerce contraire à l'interdiction.

Art. 28. Les Gouvernements signataires s'engagent également à prendre ou à proposer à leurs législatures, en cas d'insuffisance de leurs lois pénales militaires, les mesures nécessaires pour réprimer, en temps de guerre, les actes individuels de pillage et de mauvais traitements envers des blessés et malades des armées, ainsi que pour punir, comme usurpation d'insignes militaires, l'usage abusif du drapeau et du brassard de la Croix-Rouge par des militaires ou des particuliers non protégés par la présente Convention.

Ils se communiqueront, par l'intermédiaire du Conseil fédéral suisse, les dispositions relatives à cette répression, au plus tard dans les cinq ans de la ratification de la présente Convention.

Dispositions générales.

Art. 29. La présente Convention sera ratifiée aussitôt que possible.

Les ratifications seront déposées à Berne.

Il sera dressé du dépôt de chaque ratification un procès-verbal dont une copie, certifiée conforme, sera remise par la voie diplomatique à toutes les Puissances contractantes.

Art. 30. La présente Convention entrera en vigueur pour chaque Puissance six mois après la date du dépôt de ses ratifications.

Art. 31. La présente Convention, dûment ratifiée, remplacera la Convention du 22 août 1864 dans les rapports entre les États contractants.

La Convention de 1864 reste en vigueur dans les rapports entre les Parties qui l'ont signée et qui ne ratifieraient pas également la présente Convention.

Art. 32. La présente Convention pourra, jusqu'au 31 décembre prochain, être signée par les Puissances représentées à la Conférence qui s'est ouverte à Genève le 11 juin 1906, ainsi que par les Puissances non représentées à cette Conférence qui ont signé la Convention de 1864.

Celles de ces Puissances qui n'auront pas signé le 31 décembre 1906 resteront libres d'adhérer par la suite à la présente Convention. Elles auront à faire connaître leur adhésion au moyen d'une notification écrite adressée au Conseil fédéral suisse et communiquée par celui-ci à toutes les Puissances contractantes.

Les autres Puissances pourront demander à adhérer dans la même forme, mais leur demande ne produira effet que si, dans le délai d'un an à partir de la notification au Conseil fédéral, celui-ci n'a reçu d'opposition de la part d'aucune des Puissances contractantes.

Art. 33. Chacune des Parties contractantes aura la faculté de dénoncer la présente Convention ; cette dénonciation ne produira ses effets qu'un an après la notification faite par écrit au Conseil fédéral suisse et immédiatement communiquée par celui-ci à toutes les autres Parties contractantes.

Cette dénonciation ne produira ses effets qu'à l'égard de la Puissance qui l'aura notifiée.

En foi de quoi, les Plénipotentiaires ont signé la présente Convention et l'ont revêtue de leurs cachets.

Fait à Genève, le six juillet mil neuf cent six, en un seul exemplaire qui restera déposé dans les archives de la Confédération suisse, et dont des copies, certifiées conformes, seront remises par la voie diplomatique aux Puissances contractantes.

TRANSLATION.

CONVENTION FOR THE IMPROVEMENT OF THE CONDITION OF THE WOUNDED AND SICK IN ARMIES IN THE FIELD.

His Majesty the King of the United Kingdom of Great Britain and Ireland, Emperor of India, &c., &c., &c.

(*See the French text, supra, p.* 111.)

Being equally inspired by the wish to mitigate, as far as is in their power, the evils inseparable from war, and desiring, with this end in view, to perfect and complete the arrangements agreed upon at Geneva August 22, 1864, for the improvement of the condition of wounded or sick soldiers in armies in the field;

Have resolved to conclude for this purpose a new Convention, and have named as their Plenipotentiaries, that is to say:

(*See the French text, supra, p.* 111.)

Who, after having communicated to each other their full powers, found to be in good and proper form, have agreed as follows:

(*For Arts.* 1–28, *omitting Art.* 24, *see Arts.* 42–69 *of the present work.*)

The application and execution of the Convention.

Art. 24. The provisions of the present Convention are binding only upon the Contracting Powers, between two or more of them. These provisions shall cease to be binding from the moment when one of the belligerent Powers is not a Signatory of the Convention.

General Provisions.

Art. 29. The present Convention shall be ratified as soon as possible.

The ratifications shall be deposited at Berne.

When each ratification is deposited a *procès-verbal* shall be drawn up, and a copy thereof certified as correct shall be forwarded through the diplomatic channel to all the Contracting Powers.

Art. 30. The present Convention shall come into force for each Power six months after the date of the deposit of its ratification.

Art. 31. The present Convention, duly ratified, shall replace the Convention of the 22nd August, 1864, in relations between the Contracting States.

The Convention of 1864 remains in force between such of the parties who signed it who may not likewise ratify the present Convention.

Art. 32. The present Convention may be signed until the 31st December next by the Powers represented at the Conference which was opened at Geneva on the 11th June, 1906, as also by the Powers, not represented at that Conference, which signed the Convention of 1864.

Such of the aforesaid Powers as shall have not signed the present Convention by the 31st December, 1906, shall remain free to accede to it subsequently. They shall notify their accession by means of a written communication addressed to the Swiss Federal Council, and communicated by the latter to all the Contracting Powers.

Other Powers may apply to accede in the same manner, but their request shall only take effect if within a period of one year from the notification of it to the Federal Council no objection to it reaches the Council from any of the Contracting Powers.

Art. 33. Each of the Contracting Parties shall be at liberty to denounce the present Convention. The denunciation shall not take effect until one year after the written notification of it has reached the Swiss Federal Council and has been by it immediately communicated to all the other Contracting Parties.

The denunciation shall only affect the Power which has notified it.

In witness whereof the Plenipotentiaries have signed the present Convention and have affixed thereto their seals.

Done at Geneva the 6th July, 1906, in a single copy, which shall be deposited in the archives of the Swiss Confederation, and of which copies, certified as correct, shall be forwarded to the Contracting Powers through the diplomatic channel.

(*Signed for Great Britain and Ireland under reserve of Articles* 23, 27, 28.)

DÉCLARATION

RELATIVE À L'INTERDICTION DES BALLES EXPLOSIBLES EN TEMPS DE GUERRE ÉCHANGÉE À SAINT-PÉTERSBOURG, LE 11 DÉCEMBRE 1868.

Sur la proposition du Cabinet Impérial de Russie, une Commission militaire internationale ayant été réunie à Saint-Pétersbourg, afin d'examiner la convenance d'interdire l'usage de certains projectiles en temps de guerre entre les nations civilisées, et cette Commission ayant fixé d'un commun accord les limites techniques où les nécessités de la guerre doivent s'arrêter devant les exigences de l'humanité, les Sous-signés sont autorisés par les ordres de leurs Gouvernements à déclarer ce qui suit:

Considérant que les progrès de la civilisation doivent avoir pour effet d'atténuer autant que possible les calamités de la guerre;

Que le seul but légitime que les États doivent se proposer durant la guerre est l'affaiblissement des forces militaires de l'ennemi;

Qu'à cet effet il suffit de mettre hors de combat le plus grand nombre d'hommes possible;

Que ce but serait dépassé par l'emploi d'armes qui aggraveraient inutilement les souffrances des hommes mis hors de combat, ou rendraient leur mort inévitable;

Que l'emploi de pareilles armes serait dès lors contraire aux lois de l'humanité;

Les Parties contractantes s'engagent à renoncer mutuellement, en cas de guerre entre elles, à l'emploi par leurs troupes de terre ou de mer de tout projectile d'un poids inférieur à 400 grammes, qui serait ou explosible ou chargé de matières fulminantes ou inflammables.

Elles inviteront tous les États, qui n'ont pas participé par l'envoi de Délégués aux délibérations de la Commission militaire internationale réunie à Saint-Pétersbourg, à accéder au présent engagement.

Cet engagement n'est obligatoire que pour les Parties contractantes ou accédantes, en cas de guerre entre deux ou plusieurs d'entre elles; il n'est pas applicable vis-à-vis de Parties non contractantes, ou qui n'auraient pas accédé.

Il cesserait également d'être obligatoire du moment où, dans une guerre entre Parties contractantes ou accédantes, une Partie non contractante ou qui n'aurait pas accédé se joindrait à un des belligérants.

Les Parties contractantes ou accédantes se réservent de s'entendre ultérieurement toutes les fois qu'une proposition précise serait formulée en vue des perfectionnements à venir que la science pourrait apporter dans l'armement des troupes, afin de maintenir les principes qu'elles ont posés et de concilier les nécessités de la guerre avec les lois de l'humanité.

Fait à Saint-Pétersbourg
le vingt-neuf Novembre, onze Décembre, mil huit cent soixante-huit.

Pour la Grande-Bretagne . . .
ANDREW BUCHANAN.

(*The other signatory Powers were: Austria-Hungary, Bavaria, Belgium, Denmark, France, Greece, Italy, Netherlands, Persia, Portugal, Prussia and the Confederation of North Germany, Russia, Sweden and Norway, Switzerland, Turkey, Würtemberg. On* 30 *December*, 1868, *Baden, and on* 23 *October*, 1869, *Brazil, acceded to this Declaration.*)

TRANSLATION.

DECLARATION

AS TO THE PROHIBITION OF THE USE OF EXPLOSIVE BULLETS IN TIME OF WAR.

On the suggestion of the Imperial Cabinet of Russia, an International Military Commission having assembled at St. Petersburg, in order to examine into the expediency of forbidding the use of certain projectiles in time of war between civilized nations, and that Commission having by common agreement fixed the technical limits at which the necessities of war ought to yield to the requirements of humanity, the undersigned are authorized by the orders of their Governments to declare as follows:—

(*The, here omitted, six following paragraphs are set out as Articles* 71–73 *of the present work, supra, p.* 41.)

They will invite all the States which have not taken part by sending Delegates in the deliberations of the Military Commission, assembled at St. Petersburg, to accede to the present engagement.

This engagement is obligatory only upon the Contracting or Acceding Parties thereto, in case of war between two or more of them: it is not applicable with reference to non-Contracting Parties or to those which shall not have acceded to it.

It shall also cease to be obligatory from the moment when, in a war between Contracting or Acceding Parties, a non-Contracting Party, or one which has not acceded to it, shall join one of the belligerents.

The Contracting or Acceding Parties reserve to themselves to come hereafter to an understanding, whenever a precise proposal shall be made in view of future improvements which science may bring about in the arming of troops, in order to maintain the principles which they have laid down and to reconcile the necessities of war with the laws of humanity.

Done at St. Petersburg, the 29 November, 11 December, 1868.

Signed: (*See the French original*).

DÉCLARATION

RELATIVE À L'INTERDICTION DE LANCER DES PROJECTILES ET DES EXPLOSIFS DU HAUT DE BALLONS.

(October 18, 1907.)

Les Soussignés, Plénipotentiaires des Puissances conviées à la Deuxième Conférence Internationale de la Paix à La Haye, dûment autorisés à cet effet par leurs Gouvernements,

S'inspirant des sentiments qui ont trouvé leur expression dans la Déclaration de Saint-Pétersbourg du 29 novembre (11 décembre) 1868, et désirant renouveler la Déclaration de La Haye du 29 juillet 1899, arrivée à expiration,

Déclarent:

Les Puissances contractantes consentent, pour une période allant jusqu'à la fin de la Troisième Conférence de la Paix, à l'interdiction de lancer des projectiles et des explosifs du haut de ballons ou par d'autres modes analogues nouveaux.

La présente Déclaration n'est obligatoire que pour les Puissances contractantes, en cas de guerre entre deux ou plusieurs d'entre elles.

Elle cessera d'être obligatoire du moment où, dans une guerre entre des Puissances contractantes, une Puissance non contractante se joindrait à l'un des belligérants.

La présente Déclaration sera ratifiée dans le plus bref délai possible.

Les ratifications seront déposées à La Haye.

Il sera dressé du dépôt des ratifications un procès-verbal, dont une copie, certifiée conforme, sera remise par la voie diplomatique à toutes les Puissances contractantes.

Les Puissances non signataires pourront adhérer à la présente Déclaration. Elles auront, à cet effet, à faire connaître leur adhésion aux Puissances contractantes, au moyen d'une notification écrite, adressée au Gouvernement des Pays-Bas et communiquée par celui-ci à toutes les autres Puissances contractantes.

S'il arrivait qu'une des Hautes Parties Contractantes dénonçât la présente Déclaration, cette dénonciation ne produirait ses effets qu'un an après la notification faite par écrit au Gouvernement des Pays-Bas et communiquée immédiatement par celui-ci à toutes les autres Puissances contractantes.

Cette dénonciation ne produira ses effets qu'à l'égard de la Puissance qui l'aura notifiée.

En foi de quoi, les Plénipotentiaires ont revêtu la présente Déclaration de leurs signatures.

Fait à La Haye, le dix-huit octobre mil neuf cent sept, en un seul exemplaire qui restera déposé dans les archives du Gouvernement des Pays-Bas et dont des copies, certifiées conformes, seront remises par la voie diplomatique aux Puissances contractantes.

(*For the Parties to this Declaration, see Appendix IV, infra, p.* 141.)

TRANSLATION.

DECLARATION

AS TO THE PROHIBITION OF THE DISCHARGE OF PROJECTILES AND EXPLOSIVES FROM BALLOONS.

(October 18, 1907.)

The undersigned, Plenipotentiaries of the Powers invited to the Second International Peace Conference at The Hague, duly authorized by their Governments, inspired by the sentiments which found expression in the Declaration of St. Petersburg of the 29th November (11th December), 1868, and desirous of renewing the Declaration of The Hague of 29th July, 1899, which has expired,

Declare that:

(*See Art.* 73, *supra, p.* 41.)

The present Declaration is only binding on the Contracting Powers in the case of a war between two or more of them.

It shall cease to be binding from the time when, in a war between the Contracting Powers, one of the belligerents shall be joined by a non-Contracting Power.

The present Declaration shall be ratified as soon as possible.

The ratifications shall be deposited at The Hague.

A *procès-verbal* of the deposit of the ratifications shall be drawn up, and a copy of it, certified as correct, shall be sent through the diplomatic channels to all the Contracting Powers.

Non-Signatory Powers may give in their adhesion to the present Declaration. For this purpose they must make their adhesion to it known to the Contracting Powers by means of a written notification addressed to the Government of the Netherlands, and by it communicated to all the other Contracting Powers.

In the event of one of the High Contracting Parties denouncing the present Declaration, the denunciation shall not take effect until a year after the notification made in writing to the Government of the Netherlands, and forthwith communicated by it to all the other Contracting Powers.

This denunciation shall only affect the notifying Power.

In faith of which the Plenipotentiaries have signed the present Declaration.

Done at The Hague, the 18th October, 1907, in a single copy, which shall remain deposited in the archives of the Government of the Netherlands, and copies of which, certified as correct, shall be sent by the diplomatic channels to the Contracting Powers.

DÉCLARATION

CONCERNANT L'INTERDICTION DE L'EMPLOI DES PROJECTILES QUI ONT POUR BUT UNIQUE DE RÉPANDRE DES GAZ ASPHYXIANTS OU DÉLÉTÈRES.

(July 29, 1899.)

Les Soussignés, Plénipotentiaires des Puissances représentées à la Conférence Internationale de la Paix à La Haye, dûment autorisés à cet effet par leurs Gouvernements,

S'inspirant des sentiments qui ont trouvé leur expression dans la Déclaration de Saint-Pétersbourg du 29 novembre (11 décembre) 1868,

Déclarent :

Les Puissances contractantes s'interdisent l'emploi de projectiles qui ont pour but unique de répandre des gaz asphyxiants ou délétères.

(*The following eight paragraphs are identical with the corresponding paragraphs in the above Declaration as to balloons.*)

En foi de quoi, les Plénipotentiaires ont signé la présente Déclaration et l'ont revêtue de leurs cachets.

Fait à La Haye, le vingt-neuf juillet mil huit cent quatre-vingt-dix-neuf, en un seul exemplaire qui restera déposé dans les archives du Gouvernement des Pays-Bas, et dont des copies, certifiées conformes, seront remises par la voie diplomatique aux Puissances contractantes.

(*For the Parties to this and the following Declaration, see Appendix IV, infra, p.* 142.)

TRANSLATION.

DECLARATION

AS TO THE EMPLOYMENT OF PROJECTILES THE SOLE OBJECT OF WHICH IS TO DIFFUSE SUFFOCATING OR HARMFUL GASES.

(July 29, 1899.)

The undersigned, Plenipotentiaries of the Powers represented at the International Peace Conference at The Hague, duly authorized to that effect by their Governments, inspired by the sentiments which found expression in the Declaration of St. Petersburg of the 29th November (11th December), 1868,

Declare that:

(*See Art.* 74 *of this work, supra, p.* 42.)

(*As to the following eight paragraphs, see the French original.*)

In faith of which the Plenipotentiaries have signed the present Declaration, and affixed their seals thereto.

Done at The Hague, the 29th July, 1899, in a single copy, which shall be kept in the archives of the Government of the Netherlands, and copies of which, certified as correct, shall be sent through the diplomatic channels to the Contracting Powers.

DÉCLARATION

CONCERNANT L'INTERDICTION DE L'EMPLOI DE BALLES QUI S'ÉPANOUISSENT OU S'APLATISSENT FACILEMENT DANS LE CORPS HUMAIN, TELLES QUE LES BALLES À ENVELOPPE DURE, DONT L'ENVELOPPE NE COUVRIRAIT PAS ENTIÈREMENT LE NOYAU OU SERAIT POURVUE D'INCISIONS.

(July 29, 1899.)

Les Soussignés, Plénipotentiaires des Puissances représentées à la Conférence Internationale de la Paix à La Haye, dûment autorisés à cet effet pars leurs Gouvernements,

S'inspirant des sentiments qui ont trouvé leur expression dans la Déclaration de Saint-Pétersbourg du 29 novembre (11 décembre) 1868,

Déclarent :

Les Puissances contractantes s'interdisent l'emploi de balles qui s'épanouissent ou s'aplatissent facilement dans le corps humain, telles que les balles à enveloppe dure dont l'enveloppe ne couvrirait pas entièrement le noyau ou serait pourvue d'incisions.

(*The following eight paragraphs are identical with the corresponding paragraphs in the two preceding Declarations.*)

En foi de quoi, les Plénipotentiaires ont signé la présente Déclaration et l'ont revêtue de leurs cachets.

Fait à La Haye, le vingt-neuf juillet mil huit cent quatre-vingt-dix-neuf, en un seul exemplaire qui restera déposé dans les archives du Gouvernement des Pays-Bas, et dont des copies, certifiées conformes, seront remises par la voie diplomatique aux Puissances contractantes.

TRANSLATION.

DECLARATION

AS TO THE PROHIBITION OF THE USE OF BULLETS WHICH SPREAD OR FLATTEN EASILY IN THE HUMAN BODY, SUCH AS BULLETS WITH A HARD ENVELOPE, THE ENVELOPE OF WHICH DOES NOT ENTIRELY COVER THE CORE, OR IS PIERCED WITH INCISIONS.

(July 29, 1899.)

The undersigned, Plenipotentiaries of the Powers represented at the International Peace Conference at The Hague, duly authorized to that effect by their Governments, inspired by the sentiments which found expression in the Declaration of St. Petersburg of the 29th November (11th December), 1868,

Declare that :

(*See Art.* 75 *of this work, supra, p.* 42.)

(*As to the following eight paragraphs, see the French original.*)

In faith of which the Plenipotentiaries have signed the present Declaration, and have affixed their seals thereto.

Done at The Hague the 29th July, 1899, in a single copy, which shall be kept in the archives of the Government of the Netherlands, and copies of which, certified as correct, shall be sent through the diplomatic channels to the Contracting Powers.

CONVENTION No. v.

CONCERNANT LES DROITS ET LES DEVOIRS DES PUISSANCES ET DES PERSONNES NEUTRES EN CAS DE GUERRE SUR TERRE.

Sa Majesté le Roi du Royaume-Uni de Grande-Bretagne et d'Irlande, &c., &c., &c.

(*As in the Acte Final, supra, p.* 84.)

En vue de mieux préciser les droits et les devoirs des Puissances neutres en cas de guerre sur terre et de régler la situation des belligérants réfugiés en territoire neutre ;

Désirant également définir la qualité de neutre en attendant qu'il soit possible de régler dans son ensemble la situation des particuliers neutres dans leurs rapports avec les belligérants ;

Ont résolu de conclure une Convention à cet effet et ont, en conséquence, nommé pour Leurs Plénipotentiaires, savoir :

(*See the Acte Final, supra, p.* 84.)

Lesquels, après avoir déposé leurs pleins pouvoirs trouvés en bonne et due forme, sont convenus des dispositions suivantes :

CHAPITRE PREMIER. *Des Droits et des Devoirs des Puissances neutres.*

Art. 1. Le territoire des Puissances neutres est inviolable.

Art. 2. Il est interdit aux belligérants de faire passer à travers le territoire d'une Puissance neutre des troupes ou des convois, soit de munitions, soit d'approvisionnements.

Art. 3. Il est également interdit aux belligérants :

(*a*) d'installer sur le territoire d'une Puissance neutre une station radio-télégraphique ou tout appareil destiné à servir comme moyen de communication avec des forces belligérantes sur terre ou sur mer ;

(*b*) d'utiliser toute installation de ce genre établie par eux avant la guerre sur le territoire de la Puissance neutre dans un but exclusivement militaire, et qui n'a pas été ouverte au service de la correspondance publique.

Art. 4. Des corps de combattants ne peuvent être formés, ni des bureaux d'enrôlement ouverts, sur le territoire d'une Puissance neutre au profit des belligérants.

Art. 5. Une Puissance neutre ne doit tolérer sur son territoire aucun des actes visés par les Articles 2 à 4.

Elle n'est tenue de punir des actes contraires à la neutralité que si ces actes ont été commis sur son propre territoire.

Art. 6. La responsabilité d'une Puissance neutre n'est pas engagée par le fait que des individus passent isolément la frontière pour se mettre au service de l'un des belligérants.

Art. 7. Une Puissance neutre n'est pas tenue d'empêcher l'exportation ou le transit, pour le compte de l'un ou de l'autre des belligérants, d'armes, de munitions, et, en général, de tout ce qui peut être utile à une armée ou à une flotte.

Art. 8. Une Puissance neutre n'est pas tenue d'interdire ou de restreindre l'usage, pour les belligérants, des câbles télégraphiques ou téléphoniques, ainsi que des appareils de télégraphie sans fil, qui sont, soit sa propriété, soit celle de compagnies ou de particuliers.

Art. 9. Toutes mesures restrictives ou prohibitives prises par une Puissance neutre à l'égard des matières visées par les Articles 7 et 8 devront être uniformément appliquées par elle aux belligérants.

La Puissance neutre veillera au respect de la même obligation par les compagnies ou particuliers propriétaires de câbles télégraphiques ou téléphoniques ou d'appareils de télégraphie sans fil.

Art. 10. Ne peut être considéré comme un acte hostile le fait, par une Puissance neutre, de repousser, même par la force, les atteintes à sa neutralité.

Chapitre II. *Des belligérants internés et des blessés soignés chez les neutres.*

Art. 11. La Puissance neutre qui reçoit sur son territoire des troupes appartenant aux armées belligérantes les internera, autant que possible, loin du théâtre de la guerre.

Elle pourra les garder dans des camps, et même les enfermer dans des forteresses ou dans des lieux appropriés à cet effet.

Elle décidera si les officiers peuvent être laissés libres en prenant l'engagement sur parole de ne pas quitter le territoire neutre sans autorisation.

Art. 12. A défaut de convention spéciale, la Puissance neutre fournira aux internés les vivres, les habillements et les secours commandés par l'humanité.

Bonification sera faite, à la paix, des frais occasionnés par l'internement.

Art. 13. La Puissance neutre qui reçoit des prisonniers de guerre évadés les laissera en liberté. Si elle tolère leur séjour sur son territoire, elle peut leur assigner une résidence.

La même disposition est applicable aux prisonniers de guerre amenés par des troupes se réfugiant sur le territoire de la Puissance neutre.

Art. 14. Une Puissance neutre pourra autoriser le passage sur son territoire des blessés ou malades appartenant aux armées belligérantes, sous la réserve que les trains qui les amèneront ne transporteront ni personnel, ni matériel de guerre. En pareil cas, la Puissance neutre est tenue de prendre les mesures de sûreté et de contrôle nécessaires à cet effet.

Les blessés ou malades amenés dans ces conditions sur le territoire neutre par un des belligérants, et qui appartiendraient à la Partie adverse, devront être gardés par la Puissance neutre de manière qu'ils ne puissent de nouveau prendre part aux opérations de la guerre. Cette Puissance aura les mêmes devoirs quant aux blessés ou malades de l'autre armée qui lui seraient confiés.

Art. 15. La Convention de Genève s'applique aux malades et aux blessés internés sur territoire neutre.

Chapitre III. *Des personnes neutres.*

Art. 16. Sont considérés comme neutres les nationaux d'un État qui ne prend pas part à la guerre.

Art. 17. Un neutre ne peut pas se prévaloir de sa neutralité :

(*a*) s'il commet des actes hostiles contre un belligérant ;

(*b*) s'il commet des actes en faveur d'un belligérant, notamment s'il prend volontairement du service dans les rangs de la force armée de l'une des Parties.

En pareil cas, le neutre ne sera pas traité plus rigoureusement par le belligérant contre lequel il s'est départi de la neutralité que ne pourrait l'être, à raison du même fait, un national de l'autre État belligérant.

Art. 18. Ne seront pas considérés comme actes commis en faveur d'un des belligérants, dans le sens de l'Article 17, lettre *b* :

(*a*) les fournitures faites ou les emprunts consentis à l'un des belligérants, pourvu que le fournisseur ou le prêteur n'habite ni le territoire de l'autre Partie, ni le territoire occupé par elle, et que les fournitures ne proviennent pas de ces territoires ;

(*b*) les services rendus en matière de police ou d'administration civile.

CHAPITRE IV. *Du matériel des chemins de fer.*

Art. 19. Le matériel des chemins de fer provenant du territoire de Puissances neutres, qu'il appartienne à ces Puissances ou à des sociétés ou personnes privées, et reconnaissable comme tel, ne pourra être réquisitionné et utilisé par un belligérant que dans le cas et la mesure où l'exige une impérieuse nécessité. Il sera renvoyé aussitôt que possible dans le Pays d'origine.

La Puissance neutre pourra de même, en cas de nécessité, retenir et utiliser, jusqu'à due concurrence, le matériel provenant du territoire de la Puissance belligérante.

Une indemnité sera payée de part et d'autre, en proportion du matériel utilisé et de la durée de l'utilisation.

CHAPITRE V. *Dispositions finales.*

Art. 20. Les dispositions de la présente Convention ne sont applicables qu'entre les Puissances contractantes et seulement si les belligérants sont tous parties à la Convention.

Art. 21. La présente Convention sera ratifiée aussitôt que possible.

Les ratifications seront déposées à La Haye.

Le premier dépôt de ratifications sera constaté par un procès-verbal signé par les Représentants des Puissances qui y prennent part et par le Ministre des Affaires Étrangères des Pays-Bas.

Les dépôts ultérieurs de ratifications se feront au moyen d'une notification écrite adressée au Gouvernement des Pays-Bas et accompagnée de l'instrument de ratification.

Copie certifiée conforme du procès-verbal relatif au premier dépôt de ratifications, des notifications mentionnées à l'alinéa précédent, ainsi que des instruments de ratification sera immédiatement remise par les soins du Gouvernement des Pays-Bas et par la voie diplomatique aux Puissances conviées à la Deuxième Conférence de la Paix, ainsi qu'aux autres Puissances qui auront adhéré à la Convention. Dans les cas visés par l'alinéa précédent, ledit Gouvernement leur fera connaître en même temps la date à laquelle il a reçu la notification.

Art. 22. Les Puissances non signataires sont admises à adhérer à la présente Convention.

La Puissance qui désire adhérer notifie par écrit son intention au Gouvernement des Pays-Bas en lui transmettant l'acte d'adhésion qui sera déposé dans les archives du dit Gouvernement.

Ce Gouvernement transmettra immédiatement à toutes les autres Puissances copie certifiée conforme de la notification ainsi que de l'acte d'adhésion, en indiquant la date à laquelle il a reçu la notification.

Art. 23. La présente Convention produira effet, pour les Puissances qui auront participé au premier dépôt de ratifications, soixante jours après la date du procès-verbal de ce dépôt et, pour les Puissances qui ratifieront ultérieurement ou qui adhéreront, soixante jours après que la notification de leur ratification ou de leur adhésion aura été reçue par le Gouvernement des Pays-Bas.

Art. 24. S'il arrivait qu'une des Puissances Contractantes voulût dénoncer la présente Convention, la dénonciation sera notifiée par écrit au Gouvernement des Pays-Bas qui communiquera immédiatement copie certifiée conforme de la notification à toutes les autres Puissances, en leur faisant savoir la date à laquelle il l'a reçue.

La dénonciation ne produira ses effets qu'à l'égard de la Puissance qui l'aura notifiée et un an après que la notification en sera parvenue au Gouvernement des Pays-Bas.

Art. 25. Un registre tenu par le Ministère des Affaires Étrangères des Pays-Bas indiquera la date du dépôt des ratifications effectué en vertu de l'Article 21, alinéas 3 et 4, ainsi que la date à laquelle auront été reçues les notifications d'adhésion (Article 22, alinéa 2) ou de dénonciation (Article 24, alinéa 1).

Chaque Puissance contractante est admise à prendre connaissance de ce registre et à en demander des extraits certifiés conformes.

En foi de quoi, les Plénipotentiaires ont revêtu la présente Convention de leurs signatures.

Fait à La Haye, le dix-huit octobre mil neuf cent sept, en un seul exemplaire qui restera déposé dans les archives du Gouvernement des Pays-Bas et dont des copies, certifiées conformes, seront remises par la voie diplomatique aux Puissances qui ont été conviées à la Deuxième Conférence de la Paix.

TRANSLATION.

THE HAGUE CONVENTION No. v OF 1907, CONCERNING THE RIGHTS AND DUTIES OF NEUTRAL POWERS AND INDIVIDUALS IN CASE OF A WAR ON LAND.

His Majesty the King of the United Kingdom, &c., &c.

With a view to a better definition of the rights and the duties of neutral Powers in case of war on land, and to regulate the position of belligerents taking refuge in neutral Territory;

Desiring also to define the characteristics of a neutral, until it shall be possible to regulate the whole position of neutral individuals in their relations with belligerents;

Have resolved to enter into a Convention for that purpose, and have therefore named as their Plenipotentiaries, to wit:

(*As to the Powers and Plenipotentiaries, see the Acte Final, supra, p.* 84)

who, after having deposited their full powers, found to be in good and proper form, have agreed upon the following provisions:

(*Arts.* 1–19 *figure as Arts.* 121–139 *of the present work.*)

20. The provisions of the present Convention are applicable only between the Contracting Powers, and only if the belligerents are all parties to the Convention.

(*All the rest of the Convention, from Art.* 21 *to the end, is identical with H. iii, Art.* 4 *to end, and H. iv, Art.* 5 *to end, except that Art.* 25 *in this Convention varies slightly from the corresponding Articles in H. iii and H. iv, and runs as follows:*)

25. A Register kept by the Netherlands Ministry of Foreign Affairs shall give the date of the deposit of ratifications made in virtue of Art. 21, paragraphs 3 and 4, as well as the date on which the notifications of adhesion (Article 22, par. 2) or of denunciation (Article 24, par. 1) have been received.

Each Contracting Power is entitled to inspect this Register and to be supplied with extracts from it, certified as correct.

Since the Powers which are parties to the Geneva Convention of 1864 and to the Hague Convention No. ii of 1899 remain bound by those Acts, unless and until they have respectively become parties to the Geneva Convention of 1906 and to the Hague Convention No. iv of 1907, it may be desirable here to set out the terms of the earlier Geneva Convention, and to note the few, and generally unimportant, differences between the earlier and later Hague Conventions above mentioned.

The Geneva Convention of 1864.

The Swiss Confederation, H.R.H. the Grand-Duke of Baden, &c., &c., equally inspired by the wish to soften, so far as is in their power, the evils inseparable from war, to suppress useless severity, and to improve the lot of wounded soldiers on fields of battle, have resolved to conclude a Convention for this purpose, and have named as their Plenipotentiaries, to wit:

&c., &c., &c.,

who, after having exchanged their powers, found to be in good and proper form, have agreed upon the following articles:—

1. Military ambulances and hospitals shall be considered to be neutral, and, as such, shall be protected and respected by the belligerents so long as any sick or wounded shall be therein.

If these ambulances or hospitals should be held by a military force, their neutrality would terminate.

2. The persons employed in hospitals and ambulances, comprising the staff for superintendence, medical service, administration, transport of wounded, as well as the chaplains, shall share in the benefit of neutrality whilst so employed, and so long as there remain any wounded to bring in or to succour.

3. The persons mentioned in the preceding article may, even after capture by the enemy, continue to discharge their duties in the hospital or ambulance which they serve, or may withdraw in order to rejoin the corps to which they belong.

Under such circumstances, when those persons shall cease from the discharge of their duties, they shall be delivered by the army which has captured them to the outposts of the enemy.

4. As the equipment of military hospitals remains subject to the laws of war, persons attached to such hospitals cannot, on withdrawing, carry away any articles but such as are their private property.

Under the same circumstances an ambulance shall, on the contrary, retain its equipment.

5. Inhabitants of the country who shall bring help to the wounded shall be respected, and shall remain free. The Generals of the belligerent Powers shall make it their care to inform the inhabitants of the appeal addressed to their humanity, and of the neutrality which will be the consequence of it.

Any wounded man received and cared for in a house shall serve as a protection thereto. Any inhabitant who shall have taken wounded men into his house shall be exempted from the quartering of troops, as well as from a part of the war contributions which may be imposed.

6. Wounded or sick soldiers shall be brought in and cared for, to whatever nation they may belong.

Commanders-in-chief shall have the power to deliver immediately to the outposts of the enemy soldiers who have been wounded in an engagement, when circumstances permit this to be done, and with the consent of both parties.

Those who, after recovery, are considered to be incapable of serving, shall be sent back to their country.

The others may also be sent back, on consideration of not again bearing arms during the continuance of the war.

Evacuations, together with the persons under whose directions they take place, shall be protected by an absolute neutrality.

7. A distinctive and uniform flag shall be adopted for hospitals, ambulances, and evacuations. It must, in every case, be accompanied by the national flag. An arm-badge (*brassard*) shall also be allowed for individuals neutralized, but the delivery thereof shall be left to military authority.

The flag and the arm-badge shall bear a red cross on a white ground.

8. The details of the execution of the present Convention shall be regulated by the Commanders-in-chief of belligerent armies, according to the instructions of their respective Governments, and in conformity with the general principles laid down in this Convention.

9. The High Contracting Powers have agreed to communicate the present Convention to those Governments which have not been able to send Plenipotentiaries to the International Conference at Geneva, with an invitation to accede thereto ; the Protocol is for that purpose left open.

10. The present Convention shall be ratified, and the ratifications of it shall be exchanged at Berne in four months, or sooner if possible.

In witness whereof the respective Plenipotentiaries have signed the same, and have affixed thereto the seal of their arms.

Done at Geneva, the twenty-second day of August, one thousand eight hundred and sixty-four.

(Signed on behalf of twelve Powers, of which, at the time, Great Britain was not one. For a list of ratifying, or acceding Powers, see Appendix IV, p. 140.)

Differences (other than purely verbal, or as to dates) between H. ii of 1899 and H. iv of 1907.

The Convention of 1899 has been varied by that of 1907 :

in recitals, par. 4, by insertion of "have thought it necessary to complete and make clearer on certain points the work of the First Peace Conference, which ".

in par. 9, by insertion of "new" before "Convention".

by insertion, as new matter, of Arts. 3 and 4, the last two pars. of Art. 5, and Arts. 7 and 9.

The annexed *Règlement* has been similarly varied :

in Art. 2, by insertion in par. 1 of "if it bears arms openly".

in Art. 5, by insertion of "and only while circumstances necessitating this measure continue to subsist".

in Art. 6, by the insertion of, in par. 1, "with the exception of officers," and, in par. 3, "if there be no such tariff, in accordance with a tariff in proportion to the work done."

in Art. 14, by the insertion of, in par. 1, "The bureau should enter" to end, and, in par. 2, "liberated on parole, exchanged, escaped, or."

in Art. 17, by the substitution of "shall receive the pay to which officers of the same rank of the country in which they are held prisoners are entitled" for "may receive, in proper cases, the sum which is payable to them, while in that situation, by the regulations of their own country".

in Art. 23, by the addition of cl. (*h*), and of the paragraph which follows, which (except that "operations of war" is substituted for "military operations") is identical with Art. 44 of the older *Règlement*.

in Art. 25, by the insertion of "by any means whatever".

in Art. 27, by insertion of "historical monuments".

in Art. 44, by substitution of entirely new matter for that now relegated to the concluding par. of Art. 23.

in Art. 52, by addition of "and the payment of the sums due shall be made as soon as possible".

in Art. 53, par. 2, by substitution of "all the means . . . or of things" for "the material of railways, land telegraphs, steam-boats, and other vessels".

in Art. 54, by substitution of entirely new matter for the contents of the old art., which ran: "The material of railways coming from neutral States, whether belonging to those States, or to private companies or individuals, shall be returned to them as soon as possible" (see now H. v. 29, *infra* Art. 133). Arts. 57–60 of 1899 are omitted from the *Règlement* of 1907, but are textually reproduced as Arts. 11, 12, 14, 15 of H. v (*infra* Arts. 131, 132, 134, 135).

APPENDIX IV

LISTS OF POWERS WHICH ARE PARTIES (BY RATIFICATION, ACCESSION, OR AS YET MERELY BY SIGNATURE) TO THE DIPLOMATIC ACTS BEARING ON THE LAW OF WAR ON LAND.*

(1.)

Signatories of the Hague Convention No. iii of 1907, as to the commencement of hostilities (to June 30, 1908).

Argentine Republic; Austria-Hungary; Belgium; Bolivia; Brazil; Bulgaria; Chili; Colombia; Cuba; Denmark; Dominican Republic; Ecuador; France; Germany; Great Britain; Greece; Guatemala; Hayti; Italy; Japan; Luxemburg; Mexico; Montenegro; Netherlands; Panama; Paraguay; Persia; Peru; Portugal; Roumania; Russia; Salvador; Servia; Siam; Spain; Sweden; Switzerland; Turkey; United States; Uruguay; Venezuela.

* It will be observed that in the case of H. iii, iv, v, as also of the Hague Declaration of 1907, the information given relates only to the signatures appended to these Acts. It will not be possible for some time to come to give complete lists of the signatories who have ratified, and of non-signatories who have acceded to the Acts. The time allowed for signature not having expired till June 30, 1908, the Powers have had ample opportunity for deciding upon their course of action. It may therefore be presumed that the official list of signatures and reserves up to that date will almost certainly correspond to the list of ratifications which still remains to be completed.

All the Powers represented have signed, except China, Nicaragua, and Norway, and without reserve.

(2.)

SIGNATORIES OF THE HAGUE CONVENTION No. iv OF 1907, AS TO THE LAWS AND CUSTOMS OF WAR ON LAND, SUPERSEDING THAT OF 1899 ON THE SAME SUBJECT (TO JUNE 30, 1908).*

Argentine Republic; Austria-Hungary; Belgium; Bolivia; Brazil; Bulgaria; Chili; Colombia; Cuba; Denmark; Dominican Republic; Ecuador; France; Germany; Great Britain; Greece; Guatemala; Hayti; Italy; Japan; Luxemburg; Mexico; Montenegro; Netherlands; Norway; Panama; Paraguay; Persia; Peru; Portugal; Roumania; Russia; Salvador; Servia; Siam; Sweden; Switzerland; Turkey; United States; Uruguay; Venezuela.

China, Spain, and Nicaragua have not signed.

Turkey signed under reserve as to Article 3 of the Convention; and Austria-Hungary, Germany, Japan, Montenegro, and Russia, under reserve as to Article 44 of the *Règlement*.

(Parties to the Hague Convention No. ii of 1899, as to the laws and customs of war on land: now superseded as between Powers which shall have ratified the above Convention of 1907 on the same subject:—

Argentine Republic; Austria-Hungary; Belgium; Bolivia; Brazil; Bulgaria; Chili; Colombia; Corea; Cuba; Denmark; Dominican Republic; Ecuador; France; Germany; Great Britain; Greece; Guatemala; Hayti; Honduras; Italy; Japan; Luxemburg; Mexico; Montenegro; Netherlands; Nicaragua; Norway; Panama; Paraguay; Persia; Peru; Portugal; Roumania; Russia; Salvador; Servia; Siam; Spain; Sweden; Switzerland; Turkey; United States; Uruguay; Venezuela.

All these Powers, except Corea (now represented by Japan), Honduras, Nicaragua, and Spain, have already signed, and some of them have ratified, the superseding Convention of 1907.)

---

* N.B. the note to p. 138 *supra*.

(3.)

SIGNATORIES OF THE GENEVA CONVENTION OF 1906, AS TO THE CARE OF THE SICK AND WOUNDED, TOGETHER WITH POWERS WHICH HAVE ACCEDED TO IT, SUPERSEDING AS BETWEEN PARTIES TO IT THAT OF 1864 ON THE SAME SUBJECT.

Argentine Republic; *Austria-Hungary; *Belgium; *Brazil; Bulgaria; Chili; China; *Colombia; *Congo; [Corea], *Denmark; France; *Germany; *Great Britain; Greece; Guatemala; Honduras; *Italy; *Japan; *Luxemburg; *Mexico; Montenegro; Netherlands; *Nicaragua; Norway; Persia; Peru; Portugal; Roumania; *Russia; Servia; *Siam; *Spain; Sweden; *Switzerland; *Turkey; *United States; Uruguay; *Venezuela.

Great Britain signed and ratified under reserve of Arts. 23, 27, 28; Persia signed under reserve of Art. 18; and Turkey acceded under reserve that a red crescent will be employed to protect her own ambulances.

The Powers marked with * have already ratified or acceded.

(Parties to the Geneva Convention of 1864 as to the sick and wounded: now superseded, as between Powers which have ratified or acceded to the Convention of 1906 on the same subject. These Powers are marked * in the following list:—

Argentine Republic; *Austria; *Baden; *Bavaria; *Belgium; Bolivia; *Brazil; Bulgaria; Chili; China; *Colombia; *Congo; *Corea; Cuba; *Denmark; Dominican Republic; Ecuador; France; *Great Britain; Greece; Guatemala; Hayti; *Hesse-Darmstadt; Honduras; *Italy; *Japan; *Luxemburg; *Mecklenburg-Schwerin; *Mexico; Montenegro; Netherlands; *Nicaragua; Panama; Paraguay; Persia; Peru; [the Pope;] Portugal; *Prussia; Roumania; *Russia; Salvador; Saxony; Servia; *Siam; *Spain; Sweden and Norway; *Switzerland; *Turkey; *United States; Uruguay; *Venezuela; *Würtemberg.

The Pope is, of course, not now a temporal sovereign. Corea no longer exercises treaty-making powers, and many States which were separately represented in 1864 were in 1906 included in the German Empire.)

(4.)

PARTIES TO THE DECLARATION OF ST. PETERSBURG OF 1868, ON EXPLOSIVE BULLETS.

Austria-Hungary; Baden; Belgium; Brazil; Denmark; France; Great Britain; Greece; Italy; Netherlands; Persia; Portugal; Prussia; Russia; Sweden and Norway; Switzerland; Turkey.

(5, 6, 7.)

PARTIES TO THE THREE HAGUE DECLARATIONS.

i.

SIGNATORIES TO THE HAGUE DECLARATION OF 1907 AS TO PROJECTILES FROM BALLOONS (BEING A RE-DRAFT OF THE EXPIRED HAGUE DECLARATION OF 1899 ON THE SAME SUBJECT) TO REMAIN IN FORCE UNTIL THE TERMINATION OF THE THIRD PEACE CONFERENCE.*

Argentine Republic; Austria-Hungary; Belgium; Bolivia; Brazil; Bulgaria; China; Colombia; Cuba; Dominican Republic; Ecuador; Great Britain; Greece; Hayti; Luxemburg; Netherlands; Norway; Panama; Persia; Peru; Portugal; Salvador; Siam; Switzerland; Turkey; United States; Uruguay.

Chili; Denmark; France; Germany; Guatemala; Italy; Japan; Mexico; Montenegro; Nicaragua; Paraguay; Roumania; Russia; Servia; Spain; Sweden; Venezuela; have not signed.

Some of the Signatories have already ratified.

(The following Powers ratified or acceded to the Hague Declaration on this subject of 1899, which ceased to be operative at the expiration of the five years for which it was made :—

Austria-Hungary; Belgium; Bulgaria; China; Denmark; France; Germany; Greece; Italy; Japan; Luxemburg; Mexico; Montenegro; Netherlands; Persia; Portugal; Roumania; Russia; Servia; Siam; Spain; Sweden and Norway; Switzerland; United States.)

* N.B. the note to p. 138 *supra*.

---

ii.

Parties, by ratification or accession, to the Hague Declaration No. ii of 1899, as to harmful gases.

Austria-Hungary; Belgium; Bulgaria; China; Denmark; France; Germany; Great Britain; Greece; Italy; Japan; Luxemburg; Mexico; Montenegro; Netherlands; Nicaragua; Persia; Portugal; Roumania; Russia; Servia; Siam; Spain; Sweden and Norway; Switzerland.

iii.

Parties, by ratification or accession, to the Hague Declaration No. iii of 1899, as to expanding bullets.

Austria-Hungary; Belgium; Bulgaria; China; Denmark; France; Germany; Great Britain; Greece; Italy; Japan; Luxemburg; Mexico; Montenegro; Netherlands; Nicaragua; Persia; Portugal; Roumania; Russia; Servia; Siam; Spain; Sweden and Norway; Switzerland.

(8.)

Signatories of the Hague Convention No. v of 1907, as to the rights and duties of Neutrals.*

Argentine Republic; Austria-Hungary; Belgium; Bolivia; Brazil; Bulgaria; Chili; Colombia; Cuba; Denmark; Dominican Republic; Ecuador; France; Germany; Great Britain; Greece; Guatemala; Hayti; Italy; Japan; Luxemburg; Mexico; Montenegro; Netherlands; Norway; Panama; Paraguay; Persia; Peru; Portugal; Roumania; Russia; Salvador; Servia; Siam; Spain; Sweden; Switzerland; Turkey; United States; Uruguay; Venezuela.

China and Nicaragua have not signed.

The Argentine Republic signed under reserve of Art. 19, and Great Britain under reserve of Arts. 16, 17, 18.

* N.B. the note to p. 138 *supra*.

INDEX

N

O

P

Q

R

S

OXFORD
PRINTED AT THE CLARENDON PRESS
BY HORACE HART, M.A.
PRINTER TO THE UNIVERSITY

BY THE SAME AUTHOR

Albericus Gentilis, an Inaugural Lecture. London, Macmillan, 1874, 8vo. 1*s.* 6*d.*

——— tradotto da Aurelio Saffi. Roma, Loescher, 1884.

The Brussels Conference of 1874, and other diplomatic attempts to mitigate the rigour of warfare. Oxford and London, James Parker, 1876, 8vo. 1*s.* 6*d.*

The Treaty Relations of Russia and Turkey, 1774 to 1853, with an Appendix of Treaties. London, Macmillan, 1877, 12mo. 2*s.*

Alberici Gentilis De Iure Belli Libri Tres, edited. Oxford, Clarendon Press, 1877, 4to. 21*s.*

The European Concert in the Eastern Question: a Collection of Treaties and other Public Acts. Edited, with Introductions and Notes. Oxford, Clarendon Press, 1885, 8vo. 12*s.* 6*d.*

A Manual of Naval Prize Law. Issued by Authority of the Lords Commissioners of the Admiralty. London, Eyre & Spottiswoode, 1888, 8vo. 3*s.*

Studies in International Law. Oxford, Clarendon Press, 1898, 8vo. 10*s.* 6*d.*

The Laws and Customs of War on Land, as defined by the Hague Convention of 1899. Edited, with Supplementary Matter and Explanatory Notes. London, Harrison & Sons, 1904 (issued by the War Office for the information of all ranks of the British Army), 12mo. 6*d.*

Neutral Duties in a Maritime War, as illustrated by recent events (*from the Proceedings of the British Academy*). London, H. Frowde, 1905, 8vo. 1*s.*

——— traduit par E. Nys. Bruxelles, Bureau de la Revue de Droit International, 1905, 8vo.